Emotional Intelligence

Ways to Enhance Your People Skills, Social Skills, Relationships, and Self-Mastery & Boost Your EQ with Self Discipline

Table of Contents

Introduction

History of Emotional intelligence

Mixed model

The Social and Emotional Intelligence Model (ESI) by Reuven Bar-On

Emotional literacy

Criticism of the theory of emotional intelligence

The Essence Of The Concept And The Basic Theory Of Emotional Intelligence

The improved model of emotional intelligence includes 4 components:

Improving Emotional Intelligence

Emotion Diary

Control emotions

Why do we need emotions?

Measuring Emotional Intelligence

How To Recognize A Person With Emotional Intelligence

Emotional Intelligence: Managing Emotions

9 negative emotions that you must learn to manage

Emotional Intelligence and Managerial Management Style

Emotional intelligence, and why is it important?

Why is EQ more important than IQ?

Signs of high emotional intelligence

How to develop emotional intelligence

How High Emotional Intelligence Helps Work More Effectively

What is the use of EQ in the workplace

Emotional Intelligence And Managerial Leadership Style

Conclusion

Introduction

Emotional intelligence (Emotional intellect, EI) means a person's capacity to identify emotions, understand the intentions, motivation, and aspirations of others and their own, as well as the strength to maintain their feelings and emotions of separate people to solve practical problems.

The concept of emotional (social) intelligence developed as a reaction to the usual inability of traditional intelligence tests to foretell a person's success in their careers and life. This was demonstrated by the fact that successful people are competent of effective intercommunication with other people, based on emotional connections, and efficient management of their personal emotions, while the acquired concept of intelligence did not incorporate these aspects, and intelligence tests did not assess these abilities.

According to the limited scientific definition of S.J. Stein and Howard Buk, emotional intelligence, unlike the simple concept of intelligence, "is the capacity to interpret a status and influence it accurately, intuitively get what other people want and need, know their strengths and weaknesses, not to succumb to stress and be fair."

History of Emotional intelligence

It is assumed that it is the emotional intelligence in its modern understanding that was key to the survival of a person in prehistoric times, since it manifests itself in the ability to adapt to the environment, live in and find a common language with tribesmen and neighboring tribes. Charles Darwin touched this aspect in 1872 in his work "The Expression of Emotions in People and Animals," where he wrote about the role of external manifestations of emotions for survival and adaptation.

The founder of psychoanalysis Sigmund Freud dealt with the problem of emotion and control over emotions. He, in particular, believed that the first laws and prescriptions of ethics, such as the "Code of Hammurabi" (XVIII century BC, Babylon) or the edict of Emperor Ashoka, can be regarded as the first attempts to curb and civilize manifestations of emotions.

The first publications, which considered the social interaction of people as a kind of intellect, appeared long before the Second World War. In 1920, Professor Edward Thorndike first introduced the concept of social intelligence, which he described as "the ability to understand people, men, and women, boys and girls, the ability to handle people and act rationally in relationships with people." In 1926, the first widely used test (test questionnaire) was created to measure social intelligence - the George Washington Social Intelligence Test. Attempts to measure social intelligence continued in the next ten years, although, according to the conclusion Robert Thorndike (Eng. Robert Thorndike) and Saul Stern (Saul Stern), who wrote a review of methods for measuring social intelligence in 1937, these attempts were unsuccessful.

An essential contribution to the study of intelligence has made David Veksler (by David the Wechsler), who considered the intellect as "the aggregate of the individual's ability to act purposefully, to reason, also to interact effectively with the outside world." In 1940, he wrote a publication in which he divided a person's abilities into "intellectual" and "non-intellectual," among which he attributed active, personal, and social, and concluded that it was "non-intellectual" abilities that are key in predicting a person's life success. The influence of David Väckler, who was engaged in the development of intelligence tests, was also preserved at the beginning of the second half of the 20th century when it was dominant in psychology became the theory of behaviorism.

In the 1960s, the concept of emotional intelligence became the first to appear. In 1964 it appeared in the Michael Beldoka (by Michael Beldoch) Sensitivity to the emotional expression of Meaning in three modes of communication, and in 1966 by B. Loynera Emotional Intelligence and emancipation.

In 1975, Claude Steiner (born Claude Steiner), one of the founders of transactional analysis, developed the concept of emotional literacy and launched the emotional literacy training program presented in his book Achieving Emotional Literacy (ed. Avon Books, New York, 1997).

The heyday of the theory of emotional intelligence came in the 1980s and 1990s. In 1983, Howard Gardner (Howard Gardner) published his famous model of intelligence, in which he divided the intellect into intrapersonal and interpersonal. In 1985, Wayne Payne (Payne, Wayne Leon) published A Study of Emotion: Developing Emotional Intelligence, dedicated to the development of emotional intelligence. In 1988 Reuven Bar-On, in his doctoral dissertation, introduced the concept of emotional quotient the EQ (Eng. Emotional Quotient, by analogy with English. Intelligence Quotient, the IQ). Finally, in 1990, the most influential article by Peter Salovey and John Mayer [en] "Emotional Intelligence" (English Emotional Intelligence) was published, which determined the full modern understanding of emotional intelligence.

In the 1995 science journalist Daniel Goleman (by Daniel to Goleman) published a non-fiction book, Emotional Intelligence , in which he described the history of the theory of emotional intelligence, gave an overview of modern scientific concepts of emotional intelligence and even introduced its model of emotional intelligence, which later received the name of the mixed model. In 1996, Reuven Bar-On at the meeting of the American Psychological Association in Toronto presented his new EQ-i test (Emotional Quotient Inventory).), which contained a list of questions to determine the coefficient of emotional intelligence, from which the Bar-On emotional intelligence model was born.

At the inception of the XXI century, the development of the concept of emotional intelligence continued, many new publications on this topic were made by Peter Solovey (Peter Salovey), John Mayer, Howard Gardner, Konstantin Vasili Petridis. Data on the brain provision of emotional intelligence begins to accumulate.

The model of emotional intelligence Mayer-Saloveya-Caruso (model of ability)

In psychology, this model is considered to be the main one at the moment; it is usually used to describe the concept of emotional intelligence, although the mixed model of Daniel Goleman based on this model is also very. The ability model has been criticized by some scientists, in particular, Howard Gardner, for excessive psychometric bias.

Mayer, Salovey, and Caruso allocate only four components of emotional intelligence:

- The perception of emotions - the ability to recognize emotions (by facial expressions, gestures, appearance, gait, behavior, voice) of other people, as well as to identify their own emotions.

Using emotions to stimulate thinking is the ability of a person (mostly unconsciously) to activate his thinking process, to awaken creativity in himself, using emotions as a motivator.

- Understanding emotions - the ability to determine the cause of emotions, recognize the connection between thoughts and emotions, determine the transition from one emotion to another, predict the development of emotions over time, as well as the ability to interpret emotions in relationships, to understand complex (ambivalent, ambiguous) feelings.

Managing emotions is the ability to tame, awaken, and direct your emotions and the emotions of others to achieve your goals. This also includes the ability to take emotions into account when building logical chains, solving various problems, making decisions, and choosing one's behavior.

Mixed model

The model of emotional intelligence, created by scientific journalist Daniel Goleman, has gained considerable popularity due to his book, sold out in record circulation. At the same time, many scientists point to the insufficient scientific character of this model. The mixed model suggests that emotional intelligence consists of 5 components:

1. Self - knowledge is the ability to identify one's emotions, one's motivation when making decisions, to recognize one's strengths and weaknesses, to define one's goals and life values.

2. Self - regulation is the ability to control one's emotions, restrain impulses.

3. Motivation - the ability to strive to achieve the goal for the sake of its achievement.

4. Empathy - the ability to take into account the feelings of other people when making decisions, as well as the capacity to empathize with other people.

5. Social skills - the ability to build relationships with people, manipulate people, push them in the desired direction.

Three test questionnaires were created based on the Goleman model:

Emotional Competency Inventory (ECI), Emotional and Social Competency Inventory (ESCI), Emotional and Social Competency - University Edition (ESCI-U).

The Social and Emotional Intelligence Model (ESI) by Reuven Bar-On
Model Reuven Bar-On (Eng. Reuven Bar-the On) was presented at the 1996 American Psychological Association meeting in Toronto (Canada). The model consists of 15 abilities:

1.   Self - esteem is the ability to understand and evaluate yourself, see your capabilities and limitations, strengths and weaknesses, and take yourself along with your strengths and weaknesses.

2.   Emotional awareness - a person to recognize the presence of emotions in a particular moment, to distinguish their emotions and understand the causes of their occurrence.

3.   Assertiveness / Self-expression - the ability to clearly and constructively express one's feelings and thoughts, as well as the ability to mobilize one's emotional energy, to show, if necessary, the firmness of convictions, to stand on one's own.

4.   Independence - the ability to rely on yourself and not to be emotionally dependent on others.

5.   Empathy is the ability to recognize, recognize, and understand the feelings of other people.

6.   Social responsibility - the ability to identify oneself as a member of a social group, constructively cooperate with other people, take care and take responsibility for other people.

7.   Interpersonal relationships - the ability to constructive communication through verbal and non-verbal communication, the ability to establish and maintain mutually beneficial relationships based on a sense of emotional intimacy, the ability to feel free and comfortable in social contacts.

8.   Stress resistance - the ability to effectively manage your emotions, quickly find a way out of the situation.

9.   Controlling impulses - the ability to restrain their emotions, to refrain from temptation.

10. Assessment of reality - the ability to compare their thoughts and feelings with objective external reality.

11. Flexibility - the ability to instantly improve their feelings, thoughts, ideas, and behavior, according to changing circumstances.

12. Problem-solving is the ability to identify and formulate a problem, and also to find a potentially effective solution for it.

13. Self - actualization is the ability to set goals and strive to achieve them, to realize their potential.

14. Optimism - the ability to maintain hope and a positive attitude, even under challenging circumstances.

15. Happiness / Well - being is the ability to feel satisfaction with oneself, others, and life in general.

Emotional literacy

The term emotional literacy is often used in parallel, and sometimes interchangeably, with the term emotional intelligence. However, there are essential differences between them. Emotional literacy was seen as component of a project promoting humanistic education in the early 1970s.

Claude Steiner, who says that first used this term:

Emotional literacy consists of "the ability to understand your emotions, the ability to listen to others and empathize with their emotions, as well as the ability to effectively express emotions. To be emotionally literate, you need to be able to process emotions in such a way as to improve your strength and improve the quality of life around you. Emotional literacy improves relationships, creates the possibility of love between people, makes working together possible, and facilitates the emergence of a sense of community."

Steiner breaks emotional literacy into 5 parts:

1. Awareness of their feelings.

2. Possession of empathy.

3. Ability to manage your emotions.

4. Victory over emotional issues.

5.   In general: emotional interactivity.

According to Steiner, emotional knowledge is concerning understanding other people's feelings and feelings to facilitate interpersonal relationships, including through dialogue and self-control. The ability to recognize and perceive other people's feelings allows you to effectively interact with other people, as a result of which the skill of rational behavior arises in situations accompanied by strong emotions. Steiner calls this ability "emotional interactivity." Therefore, Steiner's model of emotional literacy is primarily a constructive solution to the emotional difficulties that we face to build a secure future. He concludes that personal power can be improved, and relationships modified. The importance is on the individual, and as such it strengthens the person to look inward, not on the social environment,

Criticism of the theory of emotional intelligence

Emotional intelligence is often presented as the absolute key to success in all areas of life: at school, at work, in relationships. However, according to J. Mayer, EQ is probably the cause of only 1-10% (according to other data, 2-25%) of the most essential life patterns and results. The only position in which popular and scientific concepts of emotional intelligence agreed: emotional intelligence expands ideas about what it takes to be smart.

On the other hand, all models of emotional intelligence are criticized for the somewhat arbitrary addition of components to them. And although there is no doubt that all these components really influence a person's success in life and especially in a career, but to present it as a scientific theory it is necessary to establish a specific clear principle, on the basis of which one could structure the concept of emotional intelligence, and in the absence of this principle The concept of emotional intelligence is transformed only into an arbitrary set of factors affecting a person's life.

A large amount of personal criticism was awarded to Daniel Goleman, who since the publication of his first book has been accused of a lack of a systemic scientific approach, a lack of references to sources when borrowing and of excessively commercializing the concept of emotional intelligence.

The Essence Of The Concept And The Basic Theory Of Emotional Intelligence

Today, the concept of "emotional intelligence" (Emotional Intelligence) is interpreted in different ways. There are more and less popular theories of emotional intelligence that describe the structure of EI and explain the essence of the concept. The phrase itself initially appeared in the late 20th century on the pages of academic psychological foreign literature. Today, we are already free to use this concept, because it has become an integral part of the life of modern man.

Scientists are developing new theoretical constructs, methods for diagnosing the level of emotional intelligence, practical psychologists are developing various training aimed at increasing and increasing the level of EI for people of different ages. In order to talk about EI, its importance in human life, how to train it and what methods exist for studying the level of development of EI, it is necessary to begin to understand what this concept includes, what known models of EI exist what their similarities and differences from each other are.

A person is always in a particular emotional state, which has a significant impact on his thoughts and actions. Of course, emotions are essential and represent a particular type of knowledge about oneself and about the world in which a person lives. It is on this basis - the understanding of emotions, as a particular type of knowledge, the concept of "EI" was put forward.

Over the past 20 years, psychologists have conducted a lot of research, the purpose of which is to create the complete model of EI and study its potential. Today, there are several definitions of EI, because it is not without reason that they say: how many scientists, so many opinions. Scientists will argue for a long time about what EI is, what it includes, and how much it is a scientific concept. However, initially the term "EI" included the ability to 1) process information contained in emotions, 2) determine the meaning and relationship between different emotions, 3) use the received emotional information as the basis for thinking and decision making.

In the first quater of the 20th century, David Wexler (1943) proposed the classical idea of intelligence as the global ability of an individual to act purposefully, rationally think, and effectively interact with his environment. D. Wexler distinguished between "intellectual" (rational abilities) and "non-intellectual" elements of intelligence (social, communication skills). Moreover, even though Veksler suggested that "non-intellectual" abilities are of primary importance for determining the ability of a person to achieve success, this group of factors remained almost without attention, in contrast to the cognitive component. This led to the fact that for a long time, intelligence was presented as a kind of constructor for solving logical and mathematical problems.

Back in the late 30s of the last century, Robert Thorndike put forward the concept of "social intelligence." However, the works of these authors have not been developed for a long time. And only in 1983, Howard Gardner (author of one of the modern concepts of intelligence) declared "multiple intelligence." H. Gardner identified seven forms of intelligence:

Logical and mathematical;

Verbal (linguistic);

Visual-spatial;

Body-kinesthetic;

Musical;

Interpersonal (emotional);

Spiritual (existential).

H. Gardner believed that interpersonal (emotional) intelligence and spiritual (existential) intelligence are as important as the traditionally measured IQ (verbal and logical-mathematical).

H. Gardner's concept of intelligence became the basis for the creation of the concept of, and later the first model of emotional intelligence, by John Mayer of the University of New Hampshire and Peter Salovey of Yale University.

The first model of emotional intelligence, developed by John Mayer, Peter Salovei and David Caruso in 1990, defined emotional intelligence as the capacity to recognize one's own emotions as well as the emotions of other people and use the information received to make decisions. The authors of the concept presented emotional intelligence as a construct, the components of which were abilities of 3 types:

- Ability to identify and express emotions;
- Ability to regulate emotions;
- Ability to use emotional information in thinking and activity.

The first type of ability is divided into 2 components:

1. Directed to your own emotions (it includes verbal and non-verbal subcomponents);

2. It is aimed at the emotions of other people (it includes subcomponents of non-verbal perception and empathy).

The second type of ability is also divided into 2 components:

1. Aimed at regulating their emotions;

2. Aimed at regulating the emotions of other people.

The third type of ability is divided into the following components:

1. Flexible planning;

2. Creative thinking;

3. Redirected attention;

4. Motivation.

The authors later modified the above structure of emotional intelligence. The basis for an improved version of the EI model is the idea that emotions carry information about a person's relationships with objects or other people. In the case of a change in relations with objects or other people, there is a change in the emotions that are experienced about this.

The improved model of emotional intelligence includes 4 components:
1. Identification of emotions (perception of one's emotions and emotions of other people, adequate expression of emotions, distinguishing the authenticity of emotions);

2. Understanding emotions (understanding the complexes of emotions, the relationships between emotions, the causes of emotions, verbal information

about emotions);

3. Assimilation of emotions in thinking (using emotions to direct attention to important events, the ability to evoke emotions that contribute to solving problems);

4. Management of emotions (reducing the intensity of negative emotions, solving emotionally-charged tasks without suppressing the negative emotions associated with them).

Since the works of John Mayer, Peter Salovei and David Caruso were published only in academic journals, the general public knew almost nothing about them. Daniel Goleman appreciated ideas about emotional intelligence, expanded them, and in 1995 wrote a book on emotional intelligence, which became a bestseller in the United States. This served as an impetus for the extensive study and development of this topic. In his book, D. Goleman paid particular attention to the practical application of the theory of EI in life and at work. He proposed introducing EI training programs in schools and enterprises, stating that emotional intelligence is more important than academic intelligence.

According to Goleman, the model of emotional intelligence is usually attributed to mixed models of EI. In his model of emotional intelligence, he combined cognitive abilities and personal characteristics and identified 5 main components of emotional intelligence:

1. Self-consciousness - the ability to name emotional states, the ability to understand the relationship between emotions, thinking and action, the ability to adequately assess one's strengths and weaknesses;
2. Self - regulation - the ability to control emotions, the ability to change an undesirable emotional state, the ability to recover from stress as soon as possible.
3. Motivation- the ability to enter into emotional states that contribute to success, through the use of deep-seated tendencies to take the initiative.
4. Empathy - the strength to know other people's emotions, the ability to put oneself in their place.
5. Social skills - the ability to enter into and maintain satisfying

interpersonal relationships.

D. Goleman later refined the structure of emotional intelligence. Today it consists of four components:

- Self-awareness;
- Self-control;
- Social understanding;
- Relationship management.

It is crucial to note that this structure has differences in relation to different categories of people.

According to D. Goleman, the following components and skills associated with them are essential in the development of EI leaders:

Personal skills

1. Self-awareness (Emotional self-awareness, accurate self-esteem, self-confidence);

2. Self-control (control of emotions, openness, adaptability, the will to win, initiative, optimism).

Social skills

Social sensitivity (Empathy, business awareness, helpfulness)

Relationship management (inspiration, influence, self-help, promoting change, resolving conflicts, strengthening personal relationships, teamwork, and collaboration).

As you can see, among the components of emotional intelligence, which distinguishes Goleman, there are not only emotional abilities but also social skills, strong-willed personality traits, as well as characteristics of self-awareness.

Another well-known interpretation of emotional intelligence is a model developed by Ruven Bar-On. It was Bar-He who introduced the designation EQ (emotional quotient) - the coefficient of emotionality. The author defines EQ as the totality of all non-cognitive abilities, knowledge, and competencies that allow a person to develop opportunities for solving various life problems.

The structure of emotional intelligence, according to Ruven Bar-On, is five distinct areas of competence, which include 15 abilities.

Intrapersonal sphere

Introspection;

Assertiveness

Self-esteem;

Self-actualization;

Independence.

The scope of interpersonal relationships

Empathy;

Interpersonal relationships;

Social responsibility;

Area of adaptability

Flexibility

Problem solving

Assessment of reality

Stress management

Stress resistance

Impulsiveness control

Scope of general mood

Life satisfaction

Optimism

Domestic researchers are also interested in the topic of emotional intelligence, which is being developed by such authors as D.V. Lyusin, I.I. Andreeva, D.V. Ushakov, E.A. Sergienko, O.V. Belokon, and many others.

Psychologist D.V. In 2004, Lucin proposed a new model of emotional intelligence. The author explains emotional intelligence as the ability (set of abilities) to understand and control one's and other's emotions.

The ability to understand emotions can be directed at one's emotions and the emotions of other people and means that a person:

- Can recognize emotion;
- Can identify emotion and verbalize it;
- He understands the causes of this emotion, and the consequences to which it will lead.
- The ability to manage emotions, can be directed to their emotions and the emotions of other people and means that the person:
- Can control the intensity of emotions;
- Can adjust the outward expression of emotions;
- If necessary, can arbitrarily cause this or that emotion.

The ability to understand and manage emotions, according to D.V. Lyusina is directly related to the general personal orientation to the sphere of emotions, a tendency to analyze the psychological causes of behavior, and values determined by emotional experiences.

In the concept of D.V. Lucin's "emotional intelligence" is a property of the psyche that is formed throughout life under the influence of various factors that determine its specific individual characteristics and level.

Three groups of factors can be distinguished that determine specific individual characteristics and the level of emotional intelligence:

1. Cognitive abilities (include the accuracy and speed of processing of emotional information);

2.Representations of emotions (as a valuable and essential source of information);

3. Features of emotionality (emotional stability and emotional sensitivity).

Since D.V. Lyusin does not introduce personality characteristics into the structure of emotional intelligence; this model has a fundamental difference from mixed models of emotional intelligence. The author allows only such personality characteristics that have a direct impact on individual characteristics and the level of emotional intelligence.

We have described some of the most famous models of emotional intelligence.

The first was a model by J. Mayer, P. Salovei and D. Caruso. It includes only abilities that are associated with the processing of information (cognitive abilities), in this regard, this model was defined by the authors as a model of abilities. Their theory is called "Theory of Emotional-Intellectual Abilities of Mayer J., Salovei P., Caruso D.". Then, in his theory of emotional competence, D. Goleman supplemented the model of the abilities of Salovei and Mayer, he added personality characteristics to cognitive abilities.

These types of models, in which many features are mixed that are not related to emotions and intelligence, and the main idea of emotional intelligence are mixed with many other personality traits, were called mixed models of emotional intelligence. Another mixed emotional intelligence model is Bar-She's emotional intelligence model in his non-cognitive theory of emotional intelligence. The model of emotional intelligence in the two-component theory of EI Lusin D.V. has a fundamental difference between the above models (it does not apply to either the first or the second type).

Based on the analysis of the above theories of emotional intelligence, one can define EI as a combination of the emotional and cognitive abilities of a person to its socio-psychological adaptation.

People with developed emotional intelligence, thanks to their ability to understand and manage their emotions and the emotions of other people, are well adapted in the social sphere, effective in communication and successful in achieving their goals.

Improving Emotional Intelligence

Emotional intelligence as the ability to connect with emotions to have a better life, being in touch with feelings will allow you to deal with stress levels and communicate effectively with others, two skills that improve life on a personal and professional level. Unlike IQ (intelligence quotient), which remains the same throughout life, emotional intelligence can develop and improve over time. Here, you will learn how to develop your emotional intelligence with certain techniques that you can try right now.

Connect with your emotions

Observe your emotional reactions during the day's events. It is easy to postpone feelings of what you experience on a day-to-day basis, but taking the time to recognize what your experiences make you feel is essential to improve emotional intelligence. If you ignore your feelings, you will be ignoring important information that has a great effect on your way of thinking and behaving. Start paying good attention to your feelings and relate them to your experiences.

For example, let's say you're at work, and they interrupt you during a meeting. What emotions arise in you when that happens? On the other way round, how do you feel when they congratulate you on your good work? Getting used to naming emotions such as sadness, shame, joy, satisfaction, and others will begin to raise your emotional intelligence immediately.

Get used to connecting with your emotions at certain times every day. What are your first emotions when you wake up? What are the last ones before sleeping?

Get consciousness about your body. Instead of neglecting the physical manifestations of your emotions, begin listening to them. Our minds and bodies are not separate entities; rather, they affect each other at a very deep level. You can raise your emotional intelligence by studying to interpret the signals of your body that tell you the kind of emotions you feel. For example:

- Stress may feel like a knot in the stomach, chest tightness or rapid breathing.
- The sadness could manifest when the limbs feel heavy and slow to wake up.
- Joy or pleasure may feel like butterflies in the stomach, a faster pulse or greater energy.

Discern the way your emotions and behavior are combined. When you feel heavy emotions, how do you react? Understand your internal reactions to the situations you face day by day instead of reacting without reflecting. The more you understand what prompts the impulses of your behavior, you will have higher emotional intelligence, and you can take advantage of what you know to change your behavior in the future. Here are some examples of behavior and what's behind them:

- Shame or insecurity could cause you to want to withdraw from a conversation and disconnect.

- Anger could cause you to raise the tone of your voice or get very strong footsteps.
- Feeling overwhelmed could make you panic; lose the thread of what you did, or start crying.

Avoid judging your own emotions. All your emotions are valid, even the negative ones. If you judge your emotions, you will inhibit your ability to feel full, which will make it harder for you to take advantage of your emotions in a positive way. Look at it this way: all your emotions are a new piece of useful information that is connected to some event in your world. Without that information, you would have no idea how to react properly. That's why the ability to feel emotions is a kind of intelligence.

At first, it is difficult, so you will have to practice to get your emotions afloat and connect them with what is happening. For example, if you feel bitter envy, what does that emotion tell you about your situation?

You should also experience positive emotions to the fullest. Relate your joy or satisfaction with what happens around you so you can learn to feel them more often.

Observe the presence of patterns in your emotional background. It's another way to learn as much as you can about your feelings and how they are connected to your experiences. Whenever you feel a firm emotion, ask yourself when the last time you felt it was. What happened before, during, and after?

If you observe patterns, you can exercise more control over your behavior. Observe the way you have dealt with a particular problem before and how you would like to handle it next time.

Keep a diary of your emotional reactions or how you feel every day so you can see the way you usually react.

Practice making decisions about how to behave. You cannot help but feel the emotions you feel, but you can decide how you want to react to them. If your problem is that you explode in anger or do not say anything when you are hurt, think about how you would like to react. Instead of enabling your emotions overwhelm you, decide how you want to behave the next time your feelings are very intense.

When something negative occurs in your life, take a moment to feel your emotions. Some claim to feel a wave of sadness or anger that drowns them. When the initial wave has passed, decide how you want to behave. Decide to express your feelings instead of repressing them. If you do not succeed, get up and try again instead of throwing in the towel.

Do not opt for escapist habits. It is not easy to let negative feelings come to the surface, and many people pretend to hide them by drinking too much alcohol, watching too much television or adopting other habits to hide the pain. If you do it frequently, your emotional intelligence will begin to suffer.

Connect with others

Be open-minded and be nice. Being open and pleasant goes hand in hand with emotional intelligence. A closed mind is usually an indicator of lower emotional intelligence. When you have an open mind through understanding and internal reflection, it is easier to confront conflicts in a calm and confident way. You will see that you will be more aware at a social level and new possibilities will open up for you. To strengthen that element of your emotional intelligence, take into account the following:

- Listen to contests on television or the radio. Take both sides of the argument into account and look for the subtleties that need to be analyzed in more detail.
- When a person does not react emotionally like you, reflect what could be the reason and try to see the circumstances from their point of view.

Improve your level of empathy. Empathy refers to the ability to recognize the way others feel and to share emotions with them. Being a more active listener and paying real attention to what others say will help you have a better understanding of their feelings. When you can use that information to make decisions and improve your relationships, it will be a sign of emotional intelligence.

To develop your level of empathy, place yourself in the shoes of others. Consider about how you would feel if you were in their position. Assume if you had to go through your very experiences and what could alleviate some of your deprivation in terms of support and care.

When you see someone go through a strong emotion, ask yourself: "How should I react to this same situation?"

Have a genuine interest in what others say so you can react sensitively. Instead of letting your mind wander, ask questions, and summarize what you are saying so that your interlocutor knows that you are attentive to their conversation.

Interpret the body language of others. Try to read between the lines and identify the true feelings of the people. To do so, you should observe their facial expressions and other signs of their body language. Many times people say something, but their face expresses a deeper truth, practice being more observant so that you identify the less obvious methods people use to express their emotions.

- If you're not sure you can interpret facial expressions, take a test so you can see if you can improve.
- The tone of a person's voice also says a lot. Someone with a higher tone of voice indicates that he is stressed.

Observe the effect you have on others. To raise emotional intelligence, understanding the emotions of others is half the way traveled. You will also have to understand the effect you have on others. Do you tend to make others feel nervous, happy, or angry? What happens to the conversation when you enter somewhere?

- Think of the patterns that you would have to change. If you tend to fight with your loved ones, if your girlfriend cries easily when you talk to her or if people tend to close a little when you are present, you may have to change your attitude so that you have a better emotional effect on people.
- Ask your friends or loved ones for their opinion about your emotional impact. It might be hard for you to recognize the effect you have on others; that is why they could help you.
- Practice being honest emotionally. If you say that you are "fine" but have a frown, then you will not be interacting honestly. Practice staying more physically welcoming with your emotions so that others can interpret you better. Tell them you are upset, but also share your happiness and joy.

- Being "yourself" will help others to know you and trust you more if they see where you are from.
- However, you should know that there is a limit: control your emotions, so they do not hurt others.

The practical use of emotional intelligence

See if you can improve. Being intellectually capable is crucial in life, but being emotionally intelligent has the same value. Having high emotional intelligence could give you better relationships and job opportunities. Emotional intelligence has four central elements that will help you have a balanced life. Read them and decide what you could improve on, then take the appropriate steps to practice your skills in that area:

- Self-knowledge: the ability to truly recognize one's emotions and to understand what causes them. Self-knowledge implies knowing your strengths and limitations.
- Automanejo: the ability to delay gratification, to balance your needs with those of others, to take the initiative, and to suppress impulsiveness. Self-management implies being able to deal with change and maintain a commitment.
- Social sensitivity: the ability to understand the emotions and concerns of others, as well as the ability to notice and adapt to social patterns and uses. Being aware at the social level implies being able to see the dynamics of power at play within any group or organizational context.
- Management of relationships: the ability to get along with others, to manage conflicts, to inspire and influence others, and to communicate clearly.
- Decrease your stress levels by elevating your emotional intelligence. Stress is a broad term that does refers to the anguish that is felt due to a great variety of emotions. Life is full of difficult situations, from love ruptures to job dismissals. There are a huge number of causes that trigger stress, which could turn any daily problem into something much more challenging than it is. If you are much stressed, it will be difficult to behave the way you want. Having a good plan to reduce stress will improve all aspects of your emotional intelligence.

- Find out the factors that trigger your stress and the techniques that alleviate it. Make a list of effective techniques that lower stress, such as going out with a friend or taking a walk in the forest, and then put it into practice.
- If you need help, ask for it. If your stress levels are so overwhelming that you cannot do it anymore, go to a therapist or a psychologist, who will give you the tools to cope (and at the same time help you raise your emotional intelligence).

Be more carefree at home and work. When you are optimistic, it is easier to see the beauty of life, the objects of everyday life and extend that feeling to the people around you. Optimism produces emotional well-being and greater opportunities, thanks to the fact that people want to be surrounded by optimistic people, so they will be attracted to you, without having all the possibilities that these contacts will offer you.

Negativity causes one to focus on what could go wrong instead of forging a greater capacity for recovery.

People who have high emotional intelligence tend to use humor to make others feel more secure and happy. Make use of laughter to go through difficult times.

Unlocking An Interesting Life: Emotion Diary

"What does it mean to live interestingly?" - This, in my opinion, is not so much a question of what to do in life, but of how to perceive it, from what position to relate to it.

"Living interestingly" is a certain ability, a skill that allows you to live moment by moment as fully and intensively as possible. It gives a particular quality to the life process. The fact that this opens up opportunities and realizes goals is a pleasant side effect.

From this point of view, the question "how to develop the ability to live interestingly?" becomes relevant. However, now I want to "flip" this question and ask it like this: "how to eliminate the" blocks ",

What prevents living interesting?

What kind of "blocks"? This, it seems to me, is the key point. Let's take for example some condition in which the ability to "live interestingly" is blocked - and consider how it works.

In experiencing depression, a very important role is played by the loss of interest and the ability to enjoy activities that a person previously liked. At the same time, the ability to arbitrarily direct attention changes: it "gets stuck" on negative moments, and not so much on negative moments in the present, but on painful or regrettable or nostalgic memories of the past, as well as on those images of the future with which a person is associated different fears. Add to this the bodily discomfort of chronic fatigue and muscle tightening and it turns out that being in the present moment is very difficult for a person suffering from depression.

The central element of this puzzle is the feeling "take me away from here, I'm so sick of it all, I can't feel and think these thoughts anymore." This desire is to close oneself from life, to escape from what is happening here and now, in one form or another of "time killing".

This sensation is not so much a reflection of reality as it is, but the result of passing impressions through a certain mental filter. Events take place in the outside world, we perceive them one way or another through the body, impressions arise, and then the mind comes up to them with a "measured ruler" and evaluates their compliance with their ideas about the "due." And, as a rule, it discovers one or another discrepancy, perceives this as a problem, and begins to search for a solution; in past experience, it reveals situations where a solution in similar conditions was not found; draws conclusions from this about the incompetence and incapacity of a person; extrapolates the lack of a solution to the future and makes a forecast: how exactly everything will be bad if the problem is not solved... but emotions and feelings (for example, irritation, disappointment, despondency.

This mental activity already occurs not only in isolation from the initial impression of the event from the outside world, but also in isolation from what happened in the world and in the body after this... Most people in most cases do not recognize it and continue to act in The world is "on autopilot," while attention is focused on looking at pictures from past experiences and dramatic scenarios offered by the imagination. And the "autopilot", in turn, is most often instructions drawn up in the past, and not by us.

We cease to be open to experience arising from moment to moment due to the negative feelings we experience. And these feelings, in turn, are the result of certain habits in the work of the mind - habits that we, as a rule, are not aware of. We do not enter into direct interaction with the world, because we transfer control of our own behavior to the "autopilot". This is true for most people, not just those who suffer from depression. Just by the example of depression, these blocks between a person and his ability to "live interestingly" are perhaps the most noticeable.

Mindfulness practice

In recent years, interest in the practice of mindfulness has greatly increased in the world. Initially, many hundreds of years ago, it emerged as part of the Buddhist tradition. But now it is used by those who do not consider themselves Buddhist (in particular, those who are committed to other religions and philosophies). The practice of mindfulness is aimed at disabling the autopilot and learning to turn to experience any experience with benevolent interest and based on this, make decisions.

The practice of mindfulness is a way to study the daily work of one's own mind and develop awareness that is not identified with any mental processes: "There are thoughts, feelings and sensations, they arise and pass like clouds floating through the sky. I am the sky, not the clouds "It allows you to see the habits of the mind (at least some) as a filter of perception and come into contact with the sensations and impressions of what is happening at the moment, without exposing them to interpretation and without building dramatic scenarios around them. This gives an experience of a greater fullness of life. The ability not to be identified with one's own thoughts, feelings and bodily sensations gives great freedom it becomes possible to consciously and arbitrarily plunge into this stream of contents of experience to the depth to which one wants to.

Now, mindfulness practice is considered a recognized "non-specific effectiveness factor" of psychotherapy. On its basis, therapeutic programs are created for individual and group work, which are used for patients suffering from pain and other consequences of physical trauma, from chronic diseases, from depression, etc.

Researching the workings of your own mind is more effective if accompanied by written practices. They are used in various therapeutic programs based on the practice of mindfulness, which I mentioned above. In this section I want to offer you two options for writing practice for the study of emotions.

The first option is used in a cognitive therapy program for depression. Participants are encouraged to record positive emotions on a daily basis for one week, and then on negative emotions also for one week.

 You can use diary of emotions in your first dissertation, exploring the dynamics of people's attitudes to their own emotions under the influence of observation of negative experiences and their research. This version of the diary of emotions, which I will give below. It consists of nine questions:

What situation has caused you an emotional response? Describe it briefly.

What feelings / emotions have you experienced?

If emotion could speak - what could it tell you? Or what actions prompted you to?

What thoughts arose after experiencing emotions?

How did you express your emotions?

Could emotions be expressed differently? Describe how.

How did others react to your behavior?

What experience can you relate to the positive consequences of the situation?

What experience can you relate to the negative consequences of the situation?

If you have the time and desire, first try one version of the diary of emotions, and then another, and see how the observation results differ depending on whether we focus on bodily experiences - or on the role of emotions in interacting with other people.

Control emotions

Someone is constantly being pounded by:

Hold back emotions;

Think what you do;

You do not control yourself;

You take everything to heart too close.

Someone himself has already learned to be afraid of his own emotions:

It seems to me that if I start to cry, I cannot stop;

Anger as if overshadows my eyes, I can say different things, do what I regret later;

I am so upset about trifles that then I am knocked out all day;

When I am inspired, I do not think anything, get involved in adventures, and then as if sobriety comes - how could I do such a thing.

The question of how to control our emotions faces many of us. We are afraid of actions done under the influence of emotions, not reason. They are not thought out, the consequences are not clear, which means they can be dangerous.

And if an emotion that is dangerous to us appears, we just want to get rid of it. But the reality is that if an experience was born inside, then it is impossible to turn back the clock. You can hide it from others, you can shove it deeper, so that you yourself can't see it, you can switch to positive or busy with business but to make sure that everything disappears from my soul without a trace does not work out.

And then a seemingly rational decision comes. I'm the master of my own fortunes. I will subdue them. I will make sure that they do not interfere. Hide, be distracted, switch and not notice. We enclose our emotions in slavery, we mean that we are the masters.

What will the slaves, prisoners, or any others doing something against their will do? Trying to rebel to break free is the easiest option. Some of them receive such a dose of indignation that they will try to prevail over the former owners.

And while there are not so many emotions, we manage to control them. But when the reservoir is full, when the number of suppressed experiences exceeds a certain threshold, they begin to possess more power than could be imagined. Separately, they were weak. Together they are power.

The metaphor compares the process of overflowing with emotions with a glass of vodka, poured "with a pea." The glass is full, the liquid forms a hemisphere from above, you can even take it; bring it to your lips. But if you slightly shake it or add at least one extra drop, then not only the part that was above the glass, but much more will spill out.

Around the same thing happens with our emotions. While our internal tank is able to accommodate them everything seems to be fine. But once it overflows, it is impossible to control the avalanche.

And then the moment comes in which decisions, words, actions are made not by a person, but by his emotions. What you require reto do in order to avoid such "attacks"? Maybe you should try to make friends, collaborate, and make sure that there is no war inside? But at the same time, so that people do not ricochet around? After all, lava can result in someone who is generally innocent.

If an emotion has already been born, then its only task is to be lived. Yes, for us it may not always be pleasant, but peace and tranquility inside are so desirable, right?

It is terrible to live feelings that threaten to destroy the person himself, people around him or the world as a whole. But from the fact that they scare, their task does not change. And until you give them the opportunity to manifest themselves in the world - they will not let go.

The first step, which, oddly enough, often avoids the next steps, will simply acknowledge and allow yourself to feel what is already inside. Do not run, do not hide, do not crush, do not control until destruction but see and give the opportunity to be.

This works as a sign of reconciliation and interaction in the jungle book. Do you remember? "You and I - you and I are of the same blood"

Further, most likely, it will be enough to simply say out loud the name of your condition. Call him by name.

And the next step is to ask myself what I need now in order to be able to survive (again - not to run, not to close my eyes, not to pretend that nothing is happening, but to live) this.

To be alone? Bang your fist on the wall? Swear obscenities? There will already be options that you can really control, choose, creating security for yourself and the people around you.

Of course, such a path is not a panacea. Sometimes inside us there are so many accumulated feelings that, without expressing them, reaching agreement with ourselves is impossible. In order to be able to look for safe (fashionable word - environmentally friendly) ways of expressing emotions, first you need to empty or at least to an acceptable level reduce the number of your own banned states.

Psychologist, gestalt therapist

A lot of different sayings: "But aren't emotions in my head?", "I am a rational person and proud of it, emotions are for tantrums", "Emotions prevent me from thinking", "Feelings are good when they are under strict control and don't interfere to live, "" Why talk about your feelings at all? "," Strong feelings are dangerous and destructive"... The vast majority of such thoughts were voiced by men. He returned home, I go to the Network and in front of me is a site on which a young man engaged in "self-development" actively promotes meditation and - which, unfortunately, very often goes in the middle of meditation - the fight against "destructive emotions." His site is full of the words "stop," "stop," "eliminate," "hold back," "win," "overcome", "get rid", "manage", "curb", "force", "train the ego", "tolerate", "get out of my head". He never turned to psychologists.

Another example, only from a woman, "I am too emotional and aggressive person, and this is bad, I don't know how to suppress negative emotions in me, because they prevent me and my loved ones from living, literally today, because of my violent reactions, we parted with my young man. I sobbed all day. Here again emotions. But there is no sense in tears. Nobody will help me except me. And I perfectly understand that with my cries I just hit him, so I want to learn how to control my emotions..."

Start over

In general, I will write now about emotions and why they are needed, I will try to collect basic information. I'll start a little from afar. Emotions are a mental process, and for starters it is important to explain what the psyche is. I am quite happy with this definition: the psyche is a systemic property of highly organized matter, consisting in the active reflection by the subject of the objective world and self-regulation on this basis of his behavior and activity. In other words, a living organism that has acquired the property of actively, rather than passively (like plants or simple unicellular, like amoeba) interact with the environment, reveals the presence of the psyche. The psyche does not exist separately from the nervous system and is based on the neuro-humoral (hormonal) regulation of the body's vital activity.

Imagine two conditional living cells, one of which completely dispenses with this excess, and the second acquired it. The first will be carried by the waves / wind, it will receive nutrients according to a random principle: if it is in a suitable environment, it will eat, if not, it will die; the same with danger. And the second one will begin to actively collect information from the outside world about the presence, absence of food or danger, and even before it encounters a danger or it will not respond in a direct collision with food or danger, but when it receives signals about the close presence of food / danger.

Not a single tree has escaped from the lumberjack, and the point is not only that the trees cannot run, but that they are unable to respond to the steps or the image of an approaching person with an ax... It is clear that the more complex the nervous system, the more diverse ways of interaction of the animal with the world, including such an extremely important thing as the ability to learn.

Highly Organized Matter

We are getting closer to the topic of emotion. Emotions belong to very ancient regulators of the behavior of a living organism in its interaction with the outside world. Much more ancient than our conscious thinking, which in the evolutionary sense does exist only a moment, this is a kind of pre-rational signaling system that makes the whole body aware of what is happening with it, or with the environment, and mobilizes it for action? The more developed the nervous and humoral systems of regulation, the more complicated the emotional life of a living being (it is important to remember that experiencing emotions is closely connected with hormones/neurotransmitters). Emotions work faster than a person's conscious thinking, and much more. At the same time, emotional and cognitive (cognitive) processes are a single whole, and it is impossible to tear one from the other, there is no unified theory of emotion, but what the majority converges on: emotion is a subjective experience of the body's reactions to various kinds of changes in the internal or external environment.

For example, fear can also be described purely physiologically (increased heart rate, sweating, trembling of the knees), but on a subjective level, we experience fear, and not just feel that "for some reason my knees give way." So, by the way, it happens when the conscious experience of fear is completely blocked: the body "experiences" fear, but on the subjective conscious level, "everything is in order." So, what functions do emotions perform (I will talk about human emotions)? At least three:

- Rating. For example, we experience fear when our brain, having considered all the possible information in the external environment, gives the conclusion: "Danger!" The conclusion can be based on previous experience; therefore our emotional reactions are not always adequate for the situation: a mentally healthy person with paranoid behavior, having become a hostage to the generalization (over-generalization) of his past negative experience in communicating with significant people, is now afraid of all people. Positive emotional states like joy and happiness are also associated with an assessment of how things are going. Guess why it is impossible to "turn off" negative emotions without suppressing positive ones? The function is one.

- Motivation and mobilization of energy. Emotions also motivate us to commit certain actions. If we completely turn off the emotional life of a person, then he will simply lie down and look at the ceiling there is no mobilization of energy. We all know the powerful "want!" and accompanying emotions; nervous agitation during anxiety; a strong surge of energy in anger. Emotions can motivate "from the contrary": "never again!" We are ready to go to huge lengths, just to not experience any very, very negative experiences. If we do not care, we will not do anything, because there is no energy. There is one problem with the motivational function the common law of our psyche is the struggle of motives, when directly opposed aspirations come into conflict, which is why there is a lot of energy, but it is partially used to suppress the "wrong" stimuli. The emotional situation is familiar when you want to buy something, but at the same time the price is very high, or do you need to choose one thing out of five, for example? But I really want to buy it...

- Labeling needs. Emotions are closely related to needs, and their third function (associated with the first two) is to provide a person with energy to meet a particular need and evaluate how this satisfaction occurs. For example, an unmet need for security is "marked" by fear (if the threat is obvious and understandable) or anxiety (there is a threat, but it is not clear what), fear and anxiety mobilize energy to counter the threat (most often through control). Shame indicates a bottomless hole in terms of the impossibility to satisfy the need to accept oneself by other people, anger a sudden obstacle that arose in the way of satisfying certain desires. We may not be aware of the need, but at the same time experience the emotions associated with it - this is the "labeling" of needs.

- Emotions can be simple and complex. Simple emotions are primary, simple experiences, while complex emotions are made up of a few simple ones (and they are often called "feelings"). Simple emotions include fear, anger, disgust, sadness, shame, guilt, tenderness, joy, satisfaction, curiosity, surprise, gratitude. Behind each of this emotion lies an assessment of the situation, motivation for a specific action, marking of need. Fear: danger / avoid threat / need for security. Guilt: I did something bad / atone / need to be accepted by others. Thanks: they did something good to me / to reward the benefactor / need for relationships with other people. And so on. Simple emotions can easily be translated into action.

Rational or emotional

So, an attempt to become a "rational machine" or to ignore emotions, sitting in meditation and waiting for them to "pass by themselves, the main thing is not to interfere in anything", is an attempt to ignore the ancient mechanism of self-regulation, which also works on an unconscious level (consciousness just can't keep up). Therefore, sometimes it seems to us that emotions arise by themselves, for no reason. This may be the case if you have taken psychoactive substances or have serious mental problems (with depression or schizophrenia, the balance of neurotransmitters is disturbed). Otherwise, emotions always have reasons (conscious or not), because our psyche is in continuous interaction with the environment.

Therefore, "I don't understand what has come over me, why am I annoyed at all for no reason!" - This is a direct indication that some need is not being met, and for a long time, and instead of fighting "hysteria", it would be nice to listen to what the emotion wants to communicate. However, irritation at all and everything is not an emotion, but a muddy hodgepodge / okroshka from inexperienced feelings and misunderstood own needs. As Jung said of depression: "Depression is like a lady in black. If she came, do not drive her away, but requesther to the table as a visitor, and listen to what she intends to say." Fighting emotion, we are fighting the indicator of the problem, not the problem. As if the best way to deal with a fire is to break a fire alarm or yell at a burning red light.

Do not fight with jealousy, but deal with the feeling of your own inferiority and lack of competitiveness in the fight for a partner.

How to overcome the fear of public speaking? Do not fight with fear, but figure out why the task of "please everyone present" is your priority over the task of "convey the desired information to interested listeners." Look in the face of what causes fear, and do not break the alarm.

Emotions, as I already said, do not always tell us the truth, because in the human psyche they are refracted through past experience or borrowed other people's attitudes. We can see the fire where it does not exist. But they always tell us something about our inner world, through which prism we look at our environment, and give us energy to make changes. It is important to learn how to use this wonderful tool, and not treat it like a dangerous beast, which is better put in a cage and kept on a starvation diet.

Emotional intelligence is the ability to assess and take control of your own emotions, as well as recognize the emotions of others. A person with great emotional intelligence can take advantage of their emotions when thinking and to solve problems; he manages his own emotions as well as those of others. To measure emotional intelligence, you can use standardized tests. There are questions you can ask to assess a person's emotional intelligence. If you think you do not have this ability, you can take steps to increase your emotional intelligence.

Use Tools To Measure Emotional Intelligence

Take a test online. Many online tests ensure that you measure your emotional intelligence. Usually, you will answer a series of multiple-choice questions and then present your results. You can try with the tests of this site: http://www.eiconsortium.org/measures/measures.html

Some tests are more reliable than others. The tests on this link have a substantial amount of research carried out on them, so at least they have a little more information to support them.

- Choose a test that you can take on your own to learn how you see yourself. A type of test asks you about how you see yourself. This is the simplest approach because you can do it all by yourself in less than an hour and online. However, it will not necessarily give you all the information.
- For example, this type of test may ask you to rate statements such as the following: "I get to feel annoyed often." True, Partially True or False.

Ask other people to advise you during the test. Another choice, which works well in addition to the test you can take for yourself, is to ask other people to evaluate your emotional intelligence. Essentially, they will answer questions similar to the ones you answered, but they will ask about you, giving you an idea of how other people perceive you.

- For example, the test can make a statement like the following: "This person can understand other people's emotions." True, Partially True or False.

Try it with a skills test. A third method is to use the test to verify your skills instead of just asking you to talk about them. This is beneficial because it asks you to show your emotional intelligence, which can be measured.

- This type of test can show you situations and give you answers to choose from. Alternatively, he can show you a person's face and ask you to guess the emotion he is expressing.

Look for consistent behaviors with high emotional intelligence. Emotional intelligence is not that easy to measure as other types of intelligence. However, there are general characteristics that you can observe in yourself. These characteristics tell you if you have a high level of applied emotional intelligence and include:

- Think about your emotions;
- Take breaks
- Try to control your thoughts;
- Grow thanks to criticism;
- Be authentic;
- Show empathy;
- Flatter others;
- Apologize for your mistakes;
- Keep your commitments.

Evaluate emotional intelligence in a conversation

Ask a person to describe a bad day to you and how you coped. One way to judge a person's emotional intelligence is by assessing how they deal with a situation where everything went wrong.

- For example, a person who blames others gets angry and frustrated is not emotionally aware or intelligent.

- In contrast, a flexible person who can adapt effectively and cope with difficult situations has more emotional maturity.

Talk about how you get along with other people. If you find yourself in an interview or in some other situation in which you try to assess someone else's emotional intelligence, try to get the other person to comment on their work relationships. If you do not seem to get along with anyone or if you have nothing good to say about any other person, you probably will not be as emotionally mature as you would have liked.

- For example, someone may say, "I try to maintain my professional work relationships and, to be honest, I prefer to work alone." This may indicate a lack of emotional intelligence.
- On the other hand, someone who says "I enjoy working with all kinds of people, so it makes me very happy that cooperation is encouraged in my work" may have a little more emotional maturity.

Let them teach you something. This tactic may seem a little strange, but an emotionally intelligent person will take this challenge with pleasure. Make sure you inspect the person to describe things you do not understand and see how they respond. An emotionally intelligent person will try to review what you are saying so that you can understand, while a person with less emotional intelligence will begin to feel frustrated or agitated.

Ask him who he admires. This question helps you to evaluate which values the person admires. In turn, you can see who you aspire to be, as often the people we admire are the people we aspire to be. This tells you the level of emotional intelligence for which the person is working.

Develop emotional awareness

Check your emotions throughout the day. Set the alarm to sound several times throughout the day. When you do, take a moment to review how you feel. Try to find the reason why you feel that way. The first step to having emotional awareness is to be able to recognize your emotions.

- Writing your emotions can be useful, so you can notice trends in how you feel throughout the day. However, just identifying your emotional state is useful, as it helps you to be aware of what you are feeling.

 Control your emotions. Being emotionally aware does not only reflect an emotion. You must also be able to show control over them. In a way, that means not acting because you're angry or upset. In this case, it can also mean trying to put the situation in a better perspective to help you change your emotions.

- For example, if you are upset because you received a bad review in your work, try to see it from another perspective. You can tell yourself: "This is only criticism. It's not the end of the world. I have things to learn, and this criticism will help me to do it. I have nothing left but to go forward. "
- You can also practice things like deep breathing to calm yourself down or take a break when something bothers you. For example, if you find yourself in an argument with someone and you begin to feel restless, ask to take a short break so you can calm down. Walk a little, or count slowly in your head to help you be calm.

Be a good listener when you have conversations with different people. Part of emotional awareness is being able to evaluate and understand other people's feelings. If you always feel distracted when you have conversations, likely, you are not paying attention to what the other person are talking about and feeling.

- Pay carefully attention to what the person is saying. Do not just think about what you will say. Remove or stay away from distractions such as phones, computers, and televisions, so you can focus only on what the person is saying.
- It also looks for signals that go beyond words. How is the person's tone of voice? For example, they may sound angry. What is their body language saying? Do they look agitated or nervous? If, for example, you are feeling tense, you may notice that your shoulders shrink.
- Talk about what you are seeing and hearing so that you motivate the person to open up to you. You could say, "You look a little bit anxious. Is there anything I can do to help? "

Develop your sociability. Different part of emotional intelligence is being able to take along with another people, as well as being able to negotiate, influence, lead, and handle conflicts. These skills are essential to creating bonds with other people. You can develop these skills by relating to others, so try to go to more social events that require you to interact.

- You have already learned to listen, but that is only part of sociability. You also need to communicate correctly, being direct and specific. It also assists to develop a positive attitude, as it attracts other people to you.
- For example, in a meeting, you may need to give specific instructions. "Go to work" will not be enough. Try instead: "I would like everyone to think about this project, and at the end of the day they will contact me with their ideas about how to improve it. We will meet again in two days, and by that time I would like to see some more developed suggestions.

How To Recognize A Person With Emotional Intelligence

It is a significant skill to relate and make friends with others. Whether you're watching for a new partner or a new worker, you can identify emotionally intelligent people by evaluating their interpersonal skills, paying attention to their body language, and recognizing other qualities.

Evaluate interpersonal skills

Pay attention to the person's listening ability. An emotionally intelligent person will be a skilled listener. Instead of dominating the conversation, cutting or constantly interrupting the other person while speaking, you will notice that he will listen carefully and with interest. Often, the emotionally intelligent person will summarize what the person says to indicate that he understands and hears it.

- Maybe you hear the emotionally intelligent person say things like: "From what I heard, it's not that you do not like the work, but what bothers you is the lack of communication of the staff."
- You can also control any strong emotion you may feel to communicate clearly.

Pay attention to your empathy. Emotionally intelligent people are also generally very empathetic. Empathy is explained as the ability to understand and share the feelings of others. An empathic person probably asks several questions, shows curiosity and true concern when someone is sad or has a problem. You will likely notice that this person comforts others when they cry.

- People often go to these kinds of people when they have problems and want support. Pay a close attention to the people within your circle to which others come.

Pay attention to politeness and meticulousness. Another way to identify emotionally intelligent people is to determine if they are gentle and considerate. Physical actions and verbal responses can evidence these qualities. For example, the person who usually leaves trash for others to clean up is probably not emotionally intelligent. Similarly, the person who constantly talks about how great is your partner with another co-worker who is facing a divorce probably does not have this ability.

- A person with emotional intelligence will also establish good limits. He will not try to impose himself emotionally on other people and will not take advantage of others.

Evaluate how the person talks to others. An emotionally intelligent person will avoid gossiping and talking negatively about others, unless necessary. If you often hear that person offensively insults others or notes that he tends to be in the middle of the drama, he is probably not emotionally intelligent.

- Emotionally intelligent people tend to be very honest but not necessarily discourteous.
- Although they do not talk about others negatively, they do not ignore the shortcomings or negative qualities of others.

Pay attention to how the person works and takes with others. If you work with this kind of person, you can easily assess how collaborative he is. Reflect on the times in which you have carried out projects with her and if it was an uncomplicated process.

- Pay attention to how well the person keeps their promises about delivery dates.
- Take into account if you discuss nonsense with others or manage to maintain peace.
- Pay attention to the way you deal with the change. People with emotional intelligence are more adaptable to change. They will avoid complaining, resisting, or refusing to adapt. Also, they will recognize other people's perspectives and reasons for the change.

Pay attention to the body language

Look for direct visual contact. People who have high emotional intelligence often look directly into your eyes when they talk to you to express that they are paying attention and are focused. People who have a low level of emotional intelligence look at their feet or their phones while you talk and may not even listen to what you say.

Look for a genuine smile. When a person is emotionally intelligent, he does not feel the need to fake emotions. Therefore, your expressions of happiness, sadness, or anger will be true. Keep in mind if the person you are going to evaluate shows a genuine smile.

- A genuine smile is also shown in the eyes. When someone pretends to smile, their eyes look detached from the process. A genuine smile must be expressed with the whole face.

Recognize calm gestures. You can also evaluate a person's gestures to determine if they are emotionally intelligent. People with high level of emotional intelligence will demonstrate appropriate emotions according to the context, which will not make the person with whom he speaks feel more anxious. Be careful with people who make uncontrolled and unexpected gestures or take up too much physical space by extending their hands or legs unnecessarily.

- Moving nervously is another sign of a person with low emotional intelligence.

- If a person's face is expressionless, it means that he tries to hide his true emotions. Although this may be useful in some areas, you can externalize your feelings without having to be dramatic or repressed.
- Pay attention to people who show controlled breathing. A person who resop constantly likely has no emotional intelligence.

Keep in mind if the person imitates your gestures. One of the most important signs of a person with emotional intelligence is the imitation of the posture. This behavior is defined by the act of imitating some gestures of the person with whom one speaks to convey empathy. It is done unconsciously, but it confirms that the person you are talking to actively listens to you and understands you.

- If you tilt your head to the other side, pay attention to whether the person does too.

Recognize other emotional intelligence traits

Recognize if the person has an open mind. An emotionally intelligent person is often open to the ideas and suggestions of others. Even if you do not always agree with others, at least you will recognize the validity of the thought and, at the same time, express your opinion in a respectful way.

- If this person is then willing to try new ideas, he likely has a certain degree of emotional intelligence.
- If the person is open-minded, it means that they will recognize that they do not know everything and that they do not have all the answers.

He perceives his level of self-awareness. Self-consciousness is defined as the awareness of your character, desires, and motivations. If someone tells you that they think they are honest, but you have found out lying several times recently, they may not be as self-aware. However, the person who then openly and honestly admits their strengths and weaknesses has an understanding of themselves that helps them develop their level of emotional intelligence.

Ask questions. You can assess someone's level of emotional intelligence by asking questions about their thoughts and feelings. Ask him about the ways he handles stress, who he admires or who he wants to be. That will give you an idea about your inner thoughts and desires.

- You can ask him about what he does to take care of himself when he is stressed.
- You can also ask who you turn to when faced with a difficult decision and why.

Keep in mind the way you control your emotions. A person who has a high level of emotional intelligence tends to be extremely in control of their emotions. This does not mean that these types of people are not expressive, but that they will not react or respond dramatically to circumstances that do not merit it. If a person cries over the smallest problem or throws things away when they are upset, they may not be in harmony with their emotions because they do not know how to respond appropriately.

- Pay attention and identify the person around you who, despite being emotional, maintains a calm and stable behavior.
- Also, pay attention to whether the person blames others for their emotions. People with emotional intelligence are aware that their emotions are their responsibility.

Take into account how you deal with criticism. One of the most authentic tests of emotional intelligence is to be able to handle critic with grace. People who are not that emotionally intelligent tend to shut down completely when they receive criticism or react with unwarranted intensity. Pay attention to the person who remains calm and may ask questions to understand the criticism.

- For example, someone may say that they did not complete their work well. A person with emotional intelligence can answer the following: "I admit that I could have done a more exhaustive job, but I lacked time. However, I will take your criticism into account to improve. "

1. Observe, accept and manage your emotions

The first thing we must do to improve our Emotional Intelligence is to adopt the habit of observing our reactions and behaviors. For this, it is essential to categorize in our mind some of the most habitual emotions especially those that we consider as negative or toxic, always under the premise of not condemning them or judging us for feeling them, since they do not have to be toxic in themselves. They can be considered as mere energy, and it is in our hands to channel it so that we can manage our emotions positively.

Example using Emotional Intelligence

Observing our emotions

Juan has to do an exhibition in public, when in the first he did a while ago he did not do too well. That makes her feel emotions like anxiety, anguish, or frustration. However, before the blood reaches the river, Juan stops for a moment. Take a deep breath to be more serene and observe those past experiences that are conditioning you to feel those emotions.

Accepting emotions

After his moment of reflection, Juan realizes that it is normal to feel that way. The other times that he had to expose in public, he did not feel prepared to do it for not having prepared well those exhibitions. However, now he is going to talk about a subject that he likes and that he masters perfectly, which makes him feel motivated to overcome his fears, provoking that these negative or toxic emotions are understood and accepted as part of a past that does not have to materialize in the present moment.

Managing emotions towards positive ends

After observing and accepting his emotions, Juan realizes that all this energy is making him live a very intense moment which leads him to imagine how happy he will feel about breaking down those barriers that until now were weighing on his successes. Transforming all that energy into enthusiasm, he is aware that nerves will continue to have them because he faces a significant challenge. But positively accept those nerves. Thinking that they will help you be more alert to meet your goal.

What would have happened without emotional intelligence?

If in the previous example, Juan had not managed his emotions, he would most likely have fallen into the clutches of negative thoughts. Imagining all kinds of repercussions for a possible failure, feeding this anxiety that in it was normal. Maybe to the point that would have been unattainable for him who in turn could have materialized in an exhibition in public with an insecure nonverbal language, instead of one that conveyed enthusiasm being able to stay blank no matter how well prepared the subject was.

2. Identify negative emotions

Identifying 9 emotions whose knowledge of their characteristics will help us control those emotions since our mind will have the ability to synthesize them into smaller parts.

That is, the more we know about each emotion, the less we will see them as something gross and abstract, but as steps, we can take.

Think of this metaphor: surely a mathematical integral that occupies a whole page made you very afraid to see it for the first time. But once they explained it to you and you saw that its resolution was part of a series of smaller continuous steps that fear was disappearing. Put another way; we are unable to climb a whole mountain at once. However, we are perfectly capable of walking several trails and climbing a few stretches of rock one after the other.

In this way we will go, for example, to think that we are angry and out of control (the raw result of emotions), to think that we feel anger because they have insulted us. Wondering if it deserves that we give so much value to that offense as to allow us to embitter the present moment, and it is that as the most spiritual authors defend, the conscience heals by itself.

9 negative emotions that you must learn to manage

1. Frustration

Frustration is one of the most important emotions to improve emotional intelligence. This makes us feel frustrated or disappointed with unfulfilled longings, desires, or goals. That is to say; we feel frustrated when we are not in a situation where we would like to be associating those feelings of an emotional slump with the circumstances that caused them. Their characteristics are:

- It causes anguish and can encourage us to avoid the situations that generated it.
- We tend to judge ourselves negatively damaging our self-concept.
- We blame others for not being in the situation we would like as a result of our defense mechanism.
- It is difficult for us to feel motivated in the face of new situations or challenges, no matter how different they are from those that caused us frustration.
- It encourages the exaltation of emotions such as jealousy, anguish, or shame.

2. Shame

Shame is an emotion that restrains us, undermining the confidence we need to do what we want. It causes a kind of paralysis effect, being considered by emotional intelligence as a parasite to develop our full potential. Their characteristics are:

- Constant projection towards what they can think of us.
- Beliefs of the subject that there is something bad or deficient in him.
- The tendency to avoid giving your opinions or making yourself known as it is.
- His constant repairs make him lose sight of the opportunities.
- Acts conditioned by shame usually do not fit with the talent or real abilities of individuals.
- Severe tendency to postpone the things that give her shame, never-ending them.
- Inclinations to abandon what they have learned for fear of being ridiculed.

3. Rejection

Rejection becomes toxic when we become obsessed with seeking acceptance from others. We need to control this emotion so that the value we give to ourselves is not subordinated to the opinions of others. That is, we have to learn to value ourselves from the inside for what we are. Let's see some of its characteristics:

- Constantly seek the approval of others and depend on their support to affirm themselves.
- Show off what you have for fear of rejection.
- Try to keep the rest of the people under control.
- Easily offended by negative ones and being able to respond with anger to them.
- Overestimate the opinions of others by becoming susceptible to them.
- Do not enjoy what you have if you do not receive a social value from it.
- The tendency to reject others as a result of frustration.

4. Fear

Fear is a healthy and usual emotion that drives us away from dangers. However, we often need to manage it so that this feeling of anguish does not prevent us from facing difficulties with confidence. According to Emotional Intelligence, fear becomes toxic when it paralyzes us even though we have the necessary resources to overcome it. Going back in this irrational way.

Exaggerated and circular imagination of all kinds of possible negative consequences.

·   It amplifies all other emotions, both positive and negative.

·   It paralyzes or accelerates and increases our abilities to remember those moments in which it acted.

·   Forms patterns of behavior based on past experiences: "My ex-partner already deceived me, and now I do not trust anyone."

·   It makes us concentrate too much on the past. We lose sight of the novelties of the present.

·   It has a retroactive nature: "If I'm afraid of having sex for any reason, I start to get scared to meet someone I like, I'm afraid to kiss another person for the first time, connect sexually with her, etc.... The phases before a future fear are conditioned, generating fear in them as well.

·   Reproduce mentally traumatic experiences over and over again with great detail. It is generating non-existent fears that can end up materializing in phobias.

5.   Anger or anger

Getting angry is not always bad. Sometimes it can encourage our spirit of improvement and motivate us to change things. It increases our capacity to face adverse situations (resilience). Other times it helps us to realize our mistakes. The problem comes to us when those annoyances are caused by irrelevant reasons and without which we can extract anything positive in return. Or worse still, when they make us destroy what we had.

·   It usually occurs when our expectations are not met.

·   It diminishes our ability to be empathetic and assertive.

·   It manifests itself in different levels, being able to be managed in different ways. Some release it little by little as it arrives. Others contain it and end up bursting at the least opportune moments. Others release it with forgiveness or meditation as they arrive...

·   It can be materialized in violence when levels of frustration are high.

·   It affects differently depending on the type of personality of each subject. It is usually more common in very competitive people or with a tendency to compare.

·   His verbal responses can be passive (when it is contained), assertive (when it is managed) or aggressive (when given free rein).

It usually produces feelings of guilt. Aggravating the problem or raising the awareness of the person to manage this emotion better and even taking her to ask for forgiveness.

A trick that I usually use when I feel I am getting angry is to ask myself questions that invite me to reflect. I often ask myself: Does getting angry cause me something, or will it just make me feel bad? Is Will getting upset to encourage me to get something positive in the future? Can this anger help me in some way to enjoy my current or future more?

6.   Jealousy

According to the theories on emotional intelligence, we produce jealousy when we are afraid of losing someone. It is commonly said that we can be jealous of another person because of what he or she has, but in those cases, we would be talking about a different emotion: envy.

·   They affect a relationship between two people until it becomes toxic if the jealousy is high.

·   They inhibit our feeling of feeling natural and free. What paradoxically encourages us to look for the adventure that we wanted to avoid.

·   They return to those who suffer excessively controllers or strategists.

·   They create exalted and distorted images about what the desired person can bring.

·   It can materialize in gender violence.

·   It can prevent us from appreciating and enjoying the present moment with the other person.

·   Generates dictatorial attitudes where the affected person intrudes on everything and tries to direct it.

·   Create illusory threats by seeing things that have not occurred.

·   Generates compensatory attitudes such as crying, asking for forgiveness, making gifts, etc.

The feeling of loss is what makes jealousy accentuate. Spiritual theories know how to fight this emotion very well by making us aware that we have nothing. The seduction can also help. They are providing us with security to get ahead in case of losing a current relationship, or making us feel more confident if it helps us to make a relationship work well.

7.   Emotional attachment or dependence

Managing emotions, such as attachment is vital to enjoying healthy relationships. The difficulty of controlling it lies in the shortcomings of the subject who suffers, often difficult to solve. Since the fact that a person understands, that depends on another to be happy in a clear sign of low esteem. That's why your first move ought to be to work on improving your self-esteem to learn to value yourself. Appreciating the richness of his life even when alone.

You live with many fears and frustrations thinking about how tragic life would be without the other.

- You feel that the other person is important, but you are not.

- Submission without concessions to what the other thinks or wants.

- It generates love obsessions difficult to bear and accused in tears.

- Feelings of abandonment and excessive fear to be left or set aside.

- Shyness and fear of losing the validation of the other.

- Loses consciousness and independence over one's abilities and talents.

- The constant search for others to meet their expectations also met the other way around. Feeling the responsibility to solve the problems of others.

- Feeling that life has no meaning if something is not given to others.

8. Anxiety or anguish

Emotional intelligence understands anguish as an emotion that defends us from situations that our mind perceives as dangerous. That is to say, all those that it is difficult to face. Materializing more frequently as anxiety. Being this useful to charge us with energy to face our challenges, but very harmful to health if it keeps us permanently in tension. Their characteristics are:

- Feelings of restlessness and fear, waiting for something bad to happen.

- It limits our ability to enjoy positive emotions, such as joy or love.

- It feeds doubt and perpetuates it. Continually asking ourselves what to do, what to say, or what choices to make.

- It causes us to escape or postpone situations that we should face.

- The tendency to calm this emotion with food, overwork, drugs, or medication.

9. Guilt

Feelings of guilt may be circumstantial or dragged throughout life. Feeling guilty at a specific moment when we see that we have made a mistake is healthy and normal. It's like a stop sign that tells us that this is not our way forward. However, we must manage and have this emotion well controlled when it is conditioning us negatively. That is when it causes us to act in a way that does not favor our interests; sometimes without realizing it.

·   Arabia and prevents enjoy the present moment.

·   Feel permanent debt to something or someone.

·   It torments, and these doubts can be provoked by others to manipulate us.

·   We feel that we are doing what we should.

·   It generates that the one who blames himself also demands much from others, being able to generate states of dissatisfaction.

·   The tendency to make accusations.

·   Criticism and doubt towards the actions that have been undertaken.

Torment for decisions or past experiences. Being able to embitter the present and avoiding that you can turn the page. Which, in turn, coerces the freedom of current action because of fear?

3. Manage Emotions Naturally

Bruce Lee gave us a valuable master key in that well-known interview where he told us to be like water. Be water, my friend! In it, he urged us to combine two parts in harmony: Naturalness and control. Learning to adapt to the context and identifying when we can completely abandon ourselves at the moment and when we have to use our most logical, calculating, and analytical mind to get what we want.

It takes a balance between naturalness and control

This is something that many authors have always defended at all costs, both psychologists and spiritual guides. Because we cannot forget that managing emotions is a way of encouraging control. A control that can harm our naturalness and prevent us from feeling the emotions most fully and intensely possible, let's turn into emotional accountants is neither healthy nor satisfactory! You always have to balance...

Live with a loving attitude

One way to control negative emotions consciously but in turn natural, without putting our sensitivity and spontaneity at risk, is to manage them from a loving attitude. That is, predisposing us to manage our negative emotions without abandoning the positive ones from affection, joy, and love, detaching ourselves as much as possible from the ego; the identification with the self.

4. Observe your emotions from outside

We all go through bad times and emotional imbalances. Sometimes these situations of descent are justified and indicate changes to be made in our lives. However, much of these emotional downturns have no justification whatsoever. We simply feel discouraged for no apparent reason.

This is a reality that we must accept under the risk that if we do not, we can always end up traveling on a roller coaster — encouraging emotional chaos fostered by constant self-sabotage. And the problem of self-sabotage is that it mixes a multitude of emotions in a chaotic way, being able to feel guilt, fear, frustration, anxiety, etc. All at once, according to where we are heading the vortex of our thoughts.

Talk and reflect with yourself

What I usually do is meditate seeing myself from outside in those situations, sometimes combining it with a technique more than demonstrated and as simple as talking to oneself as if we were someone else. What it would be like to do auto coaching. I say to myself: "David that you feel down now can be perfectly normal. Your life is well ordered, you are fighting for your goals, you have people who love you and value you, etc. You do not have to begin to rethink your whole life simply because you are with low spirits, because being low spirits from time to time is something natural. The bad drink passes and calm because in a few hours or a few days you will be motivated again.

5. Manage your emotions with your social skills

You do not have to be a luminary of emotional intelligence to realize that the emotions we feel depend in large part on our relationships with others. In this way, the more cultivated we have our social skills, the better we can manage our emotions.

Empathy

Improving our empathy will help us to feel what others feel. Obtaining information about your emotions and feelings, something very useful to adapt what we say to the emotional moment of others, avoiding misunderstandings and negative emotions derived from them: guilt, envy, jealousy, anxiety, fear, etc.

In turn, when we care about putting ourselves in the place of others, we begin to understand from the outside (with less implication) the emotions they are feeling. Cultivating, in this way, our capacities to observe and analyze different emotions.

Assertiveness

The assertiveness united to its most faithful ally, the empathy, of which we have already spoken, is fundamental to be able to control our emotions when we communicate. Its focus is so clear that it prevents our mind from wandering, motivated by the energy of emotions. It keeps us focused on not talking passively, which causes frustration and anxiety. Not even aggressively so as not to be filled with anger.

Emotional communication

Know how to communicate our feelings and emotions powerfully; generating empathy and understanding, makes us connect with others. Connections that cause our mind to expand attending to a multitude of possibilities, knowledge in a profound emotional way, you could say that even poetic since emotional communication is used a lot in poems.

6. Reinterpret your past through meditation

It is as essential to improve our emotional intelligence and learn to manage emotions as to heal the interpretations we have made of them in the past.

As Anthony de Mello said: "You do nothing to stop being free, you discard something. Then it is free. "To make way for the new, we must let go of the old, but it can only be released through forgiveness. It needs what psychologists call an objective revaluation of the facts, a technique that has been used within spiritual currents for thousands of years through the practice of meditation.

This technique consists in sitting down to meditate for once the thoughts are calm, entering a state of acceptance and not judgment, we begin to remember moments of our past — especially those moments where we feel bad emotionally. The idea is to look for the consequences of our behavior patterns. That is, find those past experiences that influence our current behavior. From there, once detected, we can reflect on them to give them a different approach than we had assumed in our subconscious. Giving motivating arguments that help us to free ourselves from guilt, shame, shyness... Depending on what each experience has generated and may be generating us today.

Emotions - evolutionarily earlier mechanism of regulation of behavior than the mind; therefore, they choose simple ways to solve life situations. To the one who follows their "advice," emotions add energy. Under the strong influence of emotions in the body, there is such a mobilization of forces that the mind causes neither orders nor requests.

Convinced that the struggle with emotions brings the winner more thorns than laurels, people tried to find ways of influencing their emotional world that would allow them to penetrate the underlying mechanisms of experiences and use these mechanisms more rationally than nature had.

Small joys of life are necessary to compensate for unpleasant experiences, but one should not expect deep satisfaction from their sum. It is known that children experiencing a lack of parental caress are drawn to sweets. One candy can relieve the tension of a child for some time, but even a large number of them cannot make him happier.

Each of us is somewhat reminiscent of a child who craves for candy when he tries to influence his emotions at the very moment of their occurrence. The short-term effect obtained by situational control of emotions cannot lead to stable emotional balance. This is due to the stability of the overall emotionality of a person.

The problem of human emotional culture remained relevant throughout the history of human society. Back in the Bible, in the Book of Proverbs, we find examples of the emotional wisdom of humanity: "A meek response turns away anger, and an insulting word excites"; "Slow to anger is better than the mighty, and owns a better taketh a city."

Ecclesiastes teaches: "Complaints are better than laughter; because with the grief of the face, the heart is made better." Modern philosophers, following the thinkers of antiquity, emphasize the urgency of the problem of developing emotional competence - the openness of a person to his emotional experiences, linking its possibilities with the harmonious interaction of the heart and mind, affect and intelligence.

In modern civilized society, the number of people suffering from neuroses is constantly growing. Solving the problem of emotional disorders could be facilitated by purposeful work on the development of emotional wisdom, that ability, which in modern foreign and domestic research is called emotional intelligence.

Recently, the term "emotional intelligence" has enjoyed increasing popularity.

For the first time, the designation EQ - coefficient of emotionality was introduced in 1985 by clinical physiologist Reuven Bar-On. In 1990, John Mayer and Peter Salovey introduced the concept of "emotional intelligence." Together with Daniel Goleman, the most famous in our country, these scientists make up the "top three" in the study of emotional intelligence. There are many definitions of emotional intelligence.

Reuven Bar-On, the author of the abbreviation "EQ," for example, defines emotional intelligence as "a set of non-cognitive abilities, competencies, and skills that affect a person's ability to cope with the challenges and pressures of the external environment."

Daniel Goleman - as "the ability to be aware of one's emotions and the emotions of others, to motivate oneself and others, and to manage emotions one by one with oneself and to interact with others"

Russian researcher D.V. Lucine, building on existing concepts, offers her model. He understands emotional intelligence as the ability to understand and control one's own and others'emotions.

From a psychologist, emotional intelligence is the ability to recognize one's emotions and the emotions of another, the ability to control one's emotions and the emotions of another, and to build our interaction on this basis.

High emotional intelligence in and of itself may not be a reliable predictor of success in work. However, it serves as the basis for the competencies that are necessary for success.

Emotional Competence linked to and based on emotional intelligence. A particular level of emotional intelligence is necessary for learning specific competencies related to emotions. For example, the ability to recognize what the other person feels makes it possible to develop such competencies as the ability to influence other people and inspire them.

Similarly, people who are better able to manage their emotions find it easier to develop such competencies as initiative and ability to work in a stressful situation.

It is the analysis of emotional competencies that is necessary for the prediction of success in work. It was based on mental and technical abilities that the person's prospects for success in life were evaluated. Our people before the Americans questioned the correctness of this theory, asking the question: "If you are so clever, then why so poor?"

Daniel Goleman, in his book, presented research data, according to which IQ in different versions affects the success of a person with a probability from 4 to 25%. Goleman explains this by the fact that to get into managers, you must have a certain level of IQ (IQ). You need it to go to university, for example. Therefore, all managers have a certain level of IQ. And to climb the career ladder, you need something else.

When numerous studies compared what successful managers are different from average managers, research began to point to other kinds of abilities related to understanding and managing emotions.

The theory of emotional intelligence in the first months stunned businessmen, refuting one of the main ideas of success in the twentieth century: "Emotions have no place at work." In his book, Goleman convincingly proves that people who combine intelligence and feel are most effective in their work. It is people with high emotional intelligence who make decisions better, act more effectively in critical situations, and better manage their subordinates, which, respectively, contributes to their growth through the ranks.

A hundred years before our era, the philosopher Publius Cyrus said: "Control your senses until your senses begin to govern you."

Emotions carry a huge layer of information, using which we can act much more effectively. In this case, an important point in this approach is that emotional intelligence allows you to manage your emotions. The appeal of the approach of emotional intelligence is that emotion management is a skill that can be developed and developed, which is currently confirmed by research data.

The words of the outstanding leader "Personnel decide everything" accurately describe the realities of the modern world. In the face of fierce competition, companies with competent employees are most successful. Since in managerial processes, the dominant role is played by interaction between people, competence in the sphere of interpersonal relations comes to the fore.

What abilities should a person have to build relationships with others successfully, to achieve success not only in his own life but in his professional activity?

Several studies conducted by scientists around the world show that these abilities are related to understanding and managing emotions.

In 1990, John Mayer and Peter Salovey introduced the concept of "emotional intelligence." What does this concept include?

So let's call them:

- Awareness of your emotions.

- Manage your emotions.

- Awareness of other people's emotions.

- Manage other people's emotions.

From the origin of the twentieth century, the first studies of emotionality were conducted. Since then, it is generally accepted that emotional people are different in that they take everything to heart and react violently to trifles, and the little-emotional people have enviable composure.

The well-known Soviet psychophysiologist V. D. Nebylitsyn considered emotionality to be one of the main components of a person's temperament and singled out such characteristics as impressionability, impulsivity (speed and non-thoughtfulness of emotional reactions), lability (dynamism of emotional states).

Depending on the temperament, a person with more or less intensity is emotionally involved in various situations. But if emotionality is directly related to temperament, which is based on the properties of the nervous system, then the possibility of sensibly managing emotionality without interfering with physiological processes is extremely doubtful.

Can a choleric reasonably regulate the intensity of his outbreaks if impulsiveness prevails in his temperament - a tendency toward quick and rash emotional reactions? He will have time to "break the fire" over trifles, before realizing that the most sensible principle of controlling emotions is a balance.

And a calm phlegmatic person who is not able to vividly and directly demonstrate his feelings will always be perceived by others as a person who deeply cares about what is happening. If emotionality is understood only as a combination of strength, speed of onset and mobility of emotional reactions, then for the mind there remains only one sphere of application: to accept the fact that there are emotional and unemotional people and to reckon with their natural features.

By itself, this mission of the mind is vital for human understanding. Features of temperament must be taken into account in various situations of communication. For example, you should not be offended by the violent reaction of the choleric person, which more often testifies to its impulsiveness, than to the conscious intention to offend the interlocutor.

He can be answered the same way without risking a long-lasting conflict, but even one harsh word can permanently disrupt the balance of a melancholic a vulnerable and impressionable person with a heightened sense of self-esteem.

To learn how to reasonably apply to the peculiarities of the emotional warehouse other people, not enough to know these features, you also need to be self-controlled, maintain poise no matter how intense their emotional reactions. Such an opportunity arises if, from fruitless attempts to influence directly on the intensity of emotions, a person proceeds to control situations in which emotions arise and manifests themselves.

Human emotional resources are not limitless, and if in some situations, they are spent too generously, in others; their deficit begins to be felt. Even hyperemotional people who seem to others inexhaustible in the manifestation of their feelings, being in a calm atmosphere, are plunged into a retarded state to a greater degree than those who are classified as low-emotional.

Emotions, as a rule, do not arise spontaneously, they are tied to situations and turn into steady states if the situation persists for a long time. Such emotions are called passion and the more important for a person one life situation, the higher the likelihood that one passion will crowd out all others.

Only a great passion, argued French writer Henri Petit, can take our passions. And his compatriot, writer Victor Sherbylye drew attention to the possibility of the opposite effect, arguing that our passions devour each other, and often large devour small.

It is believed that in his youth, a person is emotional, and with age, emotionality is largely lost. In fact, with the accumulation of life experience, a person expands spheres of emotional involvement, more and more situations cause him emotional associations, and, therefore, each of them causes a less intense reaction.

At the same time, the general emotionality remains the same, although in each situation observed by others the person behaves more restrained than in his youth. Of course, there are times when the ability to react violently and continuously to certain events is not lost with age. But this is typical for people of a fanatical warehouse who concentrate their emotions in one area and do not pay attention to what is happening in others.

At each moment, a person experiences some kind of emotion. Think about what kind of emotion you are experiencing at a given time (an indicator of emotions is your physical condition and internal dialogue). What is its intensity? How often does your emotion change? What are your emotions prevail?

If the answers to these questions did not cause you difficulties, it means that you are oriented in the world of your emotions. Awareness of the emotions of others involves the ability to understand the emotions that other people experience in their verbal and non-verbal behavior, and also - the ability to differentiate the true and false manifestations of the feelings of other people, to determine the change in the intensity of emotions and transitions from one emotion to another.

It is managing your emotions - the ability to determine the source and cause of emotions, its purpose, and possible consequences of development, the degree of its usefulness in a particular situation. We can regulate emotions by controlling the breath, the state of the body, using verbal and non-verbal means, controlling the internal dialogue. This ability also includes the ability to evoke the emotion needed in a particular situation. This skill helps actors to get used to the image.

And here is another example of how important it is to possess this skill. What determines the result in sports? Of course, from the skill of an athlete. Yes, but not only. How many times have we watched the failures of the strongest? "I didn't cope with excitement," said sports commentators in such cases. After all, how well an athlete knows how to own his own emotions depends largely on the result.

Will the shooter be able to hit the target, or the hand falters, can the skater cleanly perform a responsible jump, or, say, a weightlifter "take the weight"?. In training, they did it thousands of times, everything worked out in the smallest detail and brought to automatism, and at the crucial moment, nerves pass. It is not for nothing that they say that sports competitions are a competition of nerves.

Emotional competence includes the management of other people's emotions. And it implies the ability to determine the possible cause of emotion in another person and assume the consequences of its development, changing the state of another person with the help of verbal and non-verbal means; the ability to elicit the right emotion in people.

When you say a joke, you need to evoke the positive emotion of your interlocutor (verbal means). In a situation when a person experiences fear, he may not say this, everyone will say for him his facial expressions, posture, intonation (this is a non-verbal manifestation). Many talented artists, poets, musicians manage our emotions through their works.

Much has been said and written about staff motivation. But somehow it turned out that in practice the system of motivation is reduced only sometimes to a differentiated wage system: you do more and better - you get more, you do less and worse - you get less. This works, at least in most cases.

But is it enough for today? Indeed, the situation in the labor market has changed significantly in recent years.

If earlier employers chose workers from a large number of candidates, today, more and more, employees themselves choose the most suitable working conditions for themselves, the most appropriate companies. Especially if they are qualified specialists whose shortage is already well felt in the market. And high salaries and a good social package are no longer enough for them.

They choose companies where they can most fully satisfy their emotional needs: respect, recognition, status, comfort. It is noticed that the higher the social status of a person, the more attention he pays to the satisfaction of his emotional needs.

The same can be said about those who are already working in the company. It must be admitted that people decide whether they should remain in the company or not, guided solely by their emotions.

Employees remain in the company if their manager manages to create a comfortable atmosphere. And the decision is hugely emotional.

Many examples can be cited when employees left high-paying jobs only because they did not receive moral satisfaction. Conversely, they stayed at work with a low salary, if everything else was fine with them, that is, they were emotionally satisfied.

If a person feels emotional discomfort, then sooner or later, he will leave the company. If he remains, then his productivity will be very far from that which he is capable of. After all, the energy of employees, aimed at work, depends not only on the size of wages, it depends on how he feels.

It should then be noted here that the difference in the productivity of employees sometimes has nothing to do with their knowledge and skills. Everything is based on their emotional state, and the effectiveness of the work depends on what they feel, do it.

It's quite simple: if a person wants to work well, he works. If he does not want, he does not try to work and does not use his full potential. The task of motivation lies precisely in the fact that a person wants to work well. And material incentives alone are not enough here.

As practice shows, material incentives motivate quite well for some time. But sooner or later, an employee needs to be proud of his work; there is a need to recognize his merits from management and colleagues. In other words, there will be a requirement for emotional factors of motivation. And if he does not get what he wants, then his productivity will inevitably decline.

Emotional discomfort inevitably leads to a decrease in productivity. The employee simply does not see the point of working in full force. In extreme cases, such discomfort can cause overt sabotage and loss of a valuable employee for the company. In the zone of emotional comfort, people work easily, with pleasure and do an excellent job with their duties. It`s naturally. Every person subconsciously seeks positive emotions.

People learn and work best when they are in a good mood when they are interested. In this case, they mobilize their full potential. After that, they most of all want the circumstances in which they enjoyed themselves to repeat themselves.

Negative emotions, on the contrary, reduce performance, impair mental activity, reduce the ability to concentrate and, as a result, reduce productivity. No matter how hard the employee is when factors appear in his environment or his mind that prevents him from feeling good and comfortable during work, his effectiveness decreases several times, and the situation itself causes a rejection reaction.

Meanwhile, one of the major tasks of any manager is precise to utilize the full potential of its employees fully. That is what all the work on staff motivation is aimed at.

Increased productivity and, consequently, profitability - this is the result of the introduction of a competent motivation system. And here it is not possible to do without managing the emotional sphere. The manager, if he wants to be effective, must be able to manage emotions, both his own and his employees.

A capable manager, before asking the question: "How to achieve greater efficiency from subordinates?" Should ask himself the question: "How to change their emotions in the right direction for the cause?".

It would seem that everyone knows this. Indeed, there is nothing fundamentally new here. But in practice, just few people do anything in this area. Management style remains the same: instructions, directives, and instructions. The manager perceives emotional competence as something insignificant, and sometimes completely unnecessary. Well, those managers who are notified of the need for change, unfortunately, do not always know what to do.

Indeed, what can be done to make the work more interesting, exciting, stimulating activity for employees? How to create an atmosphere of trust and support? This is a difficult question.

First of all, you should stop treating employees as a working tool. The worker is not a soulless mechanism; it is a living person. And this means that he has emotions - whether we like it or not. And from what emotions he feels at work, his commitment, his productivity depends in many ways.

Managers of all ranks should understand that the ability to positively influence an employee's emotions increases the efficiency of his work, improves his relations with colleagues, and interaction with customers. The recognition of the fact of the influence of emotions on labor productivity is the first step, followed by the rest.

Human resource management must necessarily affect emotional factors. Times change, and the directive management style is gradually becoming a thing of the past. There are quite a few options for influencing the emotional sphere of employees; you just need to want to start changes in this area.

The business world is changing rapidly. The labor market is also changing. The development opportunity of any company lies in the ability to find and retain qualified specialists, talented employees.

Material incentives certainly play a big role. But emotional factors are beginning to play an increasing role. And the further, the more their role will increase. Only a comprehensive system of motivation with the mandatory consideration of the emotional component will allow employees to achieve full dedication at work, maximum efficiency, and productivity.

Managing a team of employees is one of the most critical tasks of any organization. To ensure the most excellent efficiency of its activities, along with the formal managerial functions, the manager must play the role of a motivator and moral leader, increasing the interest and ability of his subordinates, as well as maintaining an optimal atmosphere in the team.

Interest in the social and emotional aspects of work began in science back in the 20s of the last century. It was noticed that the more interest and participation the head shows in the problems of his subordinates, the higher the satisfaction of employees with their work.

Most of the competencies necessary for the success of a leader are social and emotional. In a modern organization, the leader certainly has the task of creating a favorable atmosphere in the team, directing collective emotions in the right direction, as the productivity of the group depends on the success of this function.

An effective leader not only varies the styles of his leadership, depending on the situation but is also able to apply a variety of skills associated with emotional intelligence.

Numerous studies of modern psychologists are devoted to the search for the optimal model of leadership, and most of them focus on external and group criteria for the effectiveness of leadership. In other words, the final result of the work of the whole team, including the contributions of all employees, is the criterion for the effectiveness of the activity of a manager.

Sources to highlight performance criteria can be labor productivity indicators, estimates, and personnel information. However, such signs may be associated with many other factors that relate not only to the activities of a specific manager but also to the characteristics of the organization as a whole. Also, an indicator of the effectiveness of a manager's activity is the attitude of his subordinates to each other and himself, in particular.

The successful performance of the head of his functions contributes to the improvement of psychological comfort, which includes satisfaction with the activity and its results, satisfaction with the psychological climate in the team, as well as the adequacy of professional identification and self-assessment.

At the same time, the conditions of the manager's activity and the tasks before him pose the greatest threat to maintaining psychological comfort. Thus, the head is faced with the constant assumption of responsibility, the need to continuously maintain his authority in the eyes of colleagues and subordinates, to maintain emotional contact with them.

The consequence of such working conditions may be the so-called phenomenon of emotional burnout, expressed in "dimming" of emotions, disappearance of sharpness of feelings and experiences, increase in the number of conflicts with partners in communication, indifference and isolation from the feelings of others, loss of sense of the value of life, loss of faith in their own strength.

The opposite of emotional burnout is considered a state of dedication to work. This state is characterized by vigor, energy, enthusiasm, preoccupation with activity, and a sense of effective involvement in the life of the organization. It is the dedication to work that contributes to the success of the employee's functions.

Today, most managers recognize that emotions are certainly important in building relationships with colleagues, subordinates, partners, and customers. But not everyone thinks about the influence of their emotions on daily decisions. To successfully manage their subordinates, each manager must first understand that the subordinate is "the other." In an organization, everything cannot be the same; the "other" is a managerial necessity.

If all employees are creative people, who will do the routine? Who will create a relationship in a team? If all employees are the same, then there is no resource for development. For the team to be successful, it is necessary to select their employees not for themselves, but by the task.

Ignoring the feelings of people in organizations is always dangerous, as well as neglecting any real facts. Therefore, for any manager, both own emotions and feelings of subordinates should be the object of attention.

Depending on the management strategy chosen, the manager will treat his employees differently: in one case, attention to the feelings of subordinates is necessary, as it gives a very effective tool for manipulating, in the other; feelings become one of the feedback forms, an indicator of the state of the organization.

The possibility of a regular open exchange of feelings in an organization is necessary for the manager to adjust his actions timely. An organization is an association of people who have common goals, which cannot be achieved by any of them without the assistance of others. At the same time, any person achieves his own goals: to secure for himself the necessary income, career growth, to participate in solving tasks that fully reveal his potential. The property of the human community is that all people are unique, they have different motives and goals, which mean that, in any form of association, personal interests will be objective facts in any organization. But the lack of awareness of these interests, and the inability to formulate them leads to instability in behavior, problems in business interaction.

To determine on what basis you need to build relationships with your subordinates, the head must first of all realize their personal goals and interests, answer the question: "Why do I need this organization, what do I want from it," and then help them realize the goals of their employees and choose a way to manage them in order to more effectively realize their goals, and them, and the goals of the organization as a whole.

The more styles in a manager's arsenal, the better. The best climate and the highest productivity indicators are observed in those companies whose leaders manage with the help of several styles, but with a predominance of, nevertheless, a democratic leadership style.

The most successful leaders can go almost from one style to another, depending on the situation. The greater the interest and participation in the problems of their subordinates is the head, the higher the satisfaction of employees with their work.

Emotional Intelligence In Business - A Resource That Increases Profitability By 28%

EQ or IQ - which is more important for business success?

AT

It's well known that high IQ is a set of abilities, as well as useful knowledge and skills that allow you to achieve success in your business. The significance of logical intelligence is not questioned. But logic alone is not enough for success. All her achievements are sometimes easily crossed out by a storm of human emotions. Benefits and especially formulas are often not able to win the battle with pride, envy, or anger. But emotions can be learned to control. To do this, you need to develop in yourself EQ - emotional intelligence.

Emotional intelligence, and why is it important?
EQ is a person's ability to understand people. The ability to guess their true mood (emotions), desires, motivation, and manage them. However, many entrepreneurs and top managers are not even aware of the existence of emotional intelligence, while others have successfully applied the discovery of a Yale professor for over 25 years. Obviously, a company led by a professional with a high EQ is more stable, which means it has a great competitive advantage.

The leader must develop emotional intelligence in order to:

Learn to control yourself. In difficult life circumstances, in times of stress or crisis, it is still necessary to make decisions that are important for the business, and therefore, it is necessary to maintain self-control. Important negotiations require maximum self-control. Often, one wrong phrase can ruin everything. In addition, a person who cannot cope with himself and is under stress cannot act effectively. Most of the unsuccessful decisions people make in a hurry at the moment of emotional excitement.

Improve the efficiency of your business. A statistical study conducted by the international organization CFA Institute showed that financial efficiency is almost 30% dependent on the emotional competence of company management. High EQ helps you find the best solutions in crisis situations.

Unleash your potential and capabilities. The better a person understands himself, his emotions, his strength, and his weakness, the better he can manage the available resources.

Only those who understand themselves are capable of understanding others. Who knows what he wants and how to get what he wants.

EQ in business

Business is primarily a relationship between people. Success largely depends on what kind of emotional atmosphere you manage to create. Investors, managers, employees, partners are all involved in the game of emotions. You can direct this energy to creation, or you can work in conditions of constant entropy (chaos). Skillful management of emotions can bring tremendous results.

The old Soviet approach, which denies any manifestation of emotion, is disastrous for a modern company. Therefore, the gallant slogans of those times are categorically impossible to use. Run from a business consultant who keeps repeating:

"Emotions need to be left at home. They have no place at work";

"Business is serious. There is nothing to do with emotions. "

Emotions are a unique, completely free resource, the competent use of which is capable of "moving mountains."

The development of emotional intelligence of company employees leads to:

Increase decision making speed. Red tape and red tape are a thing of the past;

Increase stress tolerance;

Increasing company flexibility in relation to counterparties. For example, understanding the emotions of a partner, you can get more favorable conditions for the supply of goods;

The cohesion of the team, which leads to an increase in labor productivity.

Why is EQ more important than IQ?

Since any business is primarily people and the relationship between them, most experts believe that EQ (emotional intelligence) is more important than IQ (logical intelligence). Indeed, the essential is always more important than formal. However, in practice, firstly, both are important, and secondly, everyone must decide for himself what he is stronger in.

For personal success, you must first develop your strengths. Of course, there should be no "white spots" either. But if we talk about the most important areas for the development of personality, then these, of course, are those in which the person is stronger, in which there is greater potential.

Regardless of their inclinations, you need to develop in yourself:

Empathy is a feeling of empathy with another person's emotional state. It would seem how this could be related to the business!? However, having observed a little, we will notice that an attentive person who understands our feelings, causes more confidence, has. Communicating with this is easy and enjoyable. Successful partnerships often grow out of "on the same wave" relationships. Empathy is no less important in business than neatness and accuracy in business and clothing;

Awareness - tracking the current emotional state without distraction to the future or past. This quality allows the entrepreneur to bring his desires as close as possible to actions and lifestyle. The more developed a person's awareness, the less he depends on random events and circumstances;

Thanks. This quality works wonders, inspiring company staff and partners to return good deeds. Know how to be grateful, and the world will turn to you its best side.

You are interested in people. It doesn't matter how sociable you are. If thinking, you think about society or specific people, you are emotionally developing. You have a high EQ, If you constantly strive to understand the actions and characters of others, if you like to get to know and learn new things about people. If you accept the fact that all people are different;

You can easily guess the emotional state of other people. A quick glance is quick enough to understand that an employee who has looked into the office is upset or confused. There is no need to ask personal questions about what happened. Most often, it's even inappropriate to ask about how to help. You just need to consider the feelings of other people. Sometimes it's enough to take a short break before moving on to an important matter. Sometimes you need to be condescending to light distraction. The circumstances are different. But one thing is always inappropriate - irritation, instead of empathy;

You can refuse. The ability to be generous, grateful must necessarily be adjacent to the ability to say no. People are responsible for their lives. Therefore, if help distracts for a long time from something significant, important, then we must refuse. If a person asks for help, because he is afraid to take up some kind of work or does not want to do it himself, one must refuse. It is effective and fair in relation to you, the employee, other employees;

You can deal with defeats. Everyone knows that failure is inevitable. Not a single success is complete without them. However, not everyone is able to cope in a fiasco without prejudice to the matter. Many improper actions greatly increase the negative effect of failure. In fact, negative emotions as a reaction to failure are natural. Ignore them is not worth it. But you need not just to get rid of thoughts of failure. It is important to use the experience gained to the benefit of the business. Failure is a ton of business-friendly information. She needs to be able to dispose of;

You know your worth well. Your own strengths and weaknesses are not a secret for you. You know how to use the former for the development of the company and manage the latter, not allowing them to interfere with the business. For example, your best employee, on which the design department is based, is absolutely tactless. A person with a low EQ will be offended and vindictively reduce each time the premium to a non-communicative introvert. What this approach will lead to is obvious. And a leader with developed EQ will help a specialist who is important for successful work to establish communication with the team. In some cases, just talking is enough. Sometimes it is advisable to attract a specialist who will help the designer and other team members to learn how to communicate. The funds here are secondary. It is important to understand the problem and have an idea of how to solve it;

You can manage your emotions. To do this, you need to learn how to determine the very emotion (sadness, anger, irritation, anxiety) and its causes. If a person is disturbed by something vague, negative, but he does not understand what it is and where it came from, he will not be able to cope. This means that it will voluntarily or involuntarily throw negative emotions on other people. At the same vein, it is important to understand that trying to completely not respond to the negative is pointless and wrong. We are inevitably offended, upset. Striving to "disconnect" living human reactions is not necessary. It is important to be able to react correctly. If an employee negatively commented on innovation in the company, you should try to understand the reasons for the dissatisfaction. Having figured out what the problem is, it can be easily solved. If employees show poorly disguised discontent,

You can neutralize negative people. Alas, without special training, it is almost impossible to control the situation when dealing with toxic people. An untrained person will quickly give up the situation to the power of irritation and other negative emotions of his own. A manager with a high EQ is able to cope with the temptations and not respond to the illogical behavior of a negative employee;

You find the opportunity to notice the people around you, their emotions, even if you yourself are very busy or in a hurry. You always have a couple of minutes to help other people, no matter how hard you are in a hurry;

You are adaptive. Easy adaptation to constantly changing conditions is a necessary quality of a modern entrepreneur. If he stops changing, the world does not stop changing with him. Therefore, his company will gradually lose its position, less and less in line with the situation. Unwillingness to accept the new always hinders development. Another thing is that business strategy and tactics may be different. It's not necessary to implement the latest. Sometimes it is better to give this path to others and to follow the beaten track;

You know how to relax. To give a lot, you need to get a lot of energy. She is born from relaxation and human communication. Both that and another, it is necessary to learn to do profitably. If there is no time for leisure at all, and it happens, you need to relieve stress by various techniques. People with high EQ know how to strike a balance between work and leisure. It is important to learn how to extract energy from work to rest, and not to continue at home, like a hare-energizer, to think and talk about business;

You can listen. A person with high emotional intelligence understands the feelings and emotions of others, not only through the text but also through what is in pauses;

You can set realistic goals. The disease of the 20th-century generation is perfectionism. Many are simply not able to complete any business, as they endlessly strive for the best. It is important to learn how to achieve your goals on time, even if something comes first at C grade. If a mediocre result is always obtained, you have to think about whether the case is chosen. You need to take it not for what is successful, profitable, popular, but for what works better than others. Not perfect, but better.

This is not a complete list of qualities that make it possible to reveal all the facets of emotional intelligence. Different people have different abilities. Possess all the virtues, including all of the above, impossible.

How to develop emotional intelligence

To develop or even constantly develop EQ, you need to make efforts to acquire the qualities inherent in people with highly developed emotional intelligence. We described these features above. Let us dwell on some of them in more detail.

Learning to understand yourself

Obviously, the path to understanding others lies through understanding oneself. As soon as there is clarity with oneself, one can try to put oneself in the circumstances of other people. It is important not only to put yourself in the place of another person. It's not easy to evaluate what you would do in a given situation. It is important to try to understand how you would act, how you felt in a particular situation, but as a different person. Imagine that you are not a successful director of the company, but a novice specialist. Financial difficulties. A crying little child who keeps you awake, perhaps a part-time job or your own small business on the Internet, giving hope for an improvement in the financial situation in the future, what can you offer such an employee to motivate him to spend his free time and energy on the development of your company? It makes no sense to scold and punish the desire to have more. We need to give incentives for growth.

Psychology of manifestation or psychology of gestures

You can guess the emotions of the interlocutor by external manifestations. Annoyance or sadness, joy, or boredom is manifested equally in different people. A person has many means that allow expressing the same feeling, but all people use the same set. Therefore, knowing the psychology of gestures or, as they sometimes say, the psychology of manifestation, one can guess emotions. For example, wide-open eyes and a deep breath usually speak of surprise. It is not necessary to memorize a list of signs that allows you to identify a particular emotion. It is enough to be observant. The skill of observation also needs to be developed in oneself.

The psychology of manifestation allows you to master the art of understanding gestures, repeating them. If you accept the same position as the interlocutor, then you will experience the same feelings. Assessment should be made taking into account the relevance, adequacy, strength of manifestation, and tension. The main difficulty is that repeating everything exactly is not so simple. To learn, you need to practice for a long time. First, gestures are repeated literally, physically, then it will be enough to do it mentally.

As you can see, the development of emotional intelligence opens up many opportunities for a businessman. Not to use this pantry means to doom yourself to a notorious loss in the competition.

How High Emotional Intelligence Helps Work More Effectively

Is it true that emotions have no place at work? Many answers in the affirmative, but emotional feelings do not go away from this. Therefore, the correct formulation of the question will be this: why is it important to manage emotions in the work team?

Why do people need emotions

Emotions are mental processes that are a reaction to external circumstances. This can be seen in the behavior of children who begin to scream and stomp their feet if something causes them anger and a feeling of protest. Adults experience the same feelings, but they are able to consciously choose strategies for behavior, instead of immediately moving on to actions.

Emotions provide us with quick, but sometimes too peremptory action programs. In primitive times, this could save a person's life. However, in our time, the world has become much more complicated, and in order to cope with a problem, you can't just run away from it or get into a fight.

To react in an "emotionally smart" way, you need to realize what happened, accept your experience, and direct your energy to what you can influence. In addition, developing social and emotional skills allow you to build relationships with others successfully.

Emotional intelligence today falls into all kinds of lists of competencies of the 21st century, without which the labor market cannot do in the future. He is attributed to tosoft, or non-cognitive skills. That is, those are associated with interhuman interactions and are needed in any area of professional activity, regardless of whether you are engaged in software development or work as a chef.

What is the use of EQ in the workplace

Emotional intelligence can be either individual or common to a particular company or work team - this is called the collective emotional factor.

According to the American specialist in the field of labor organization, Judy Bell, teams in which EQ is high have higher productivity, because the specialists interact better with each other. In companies where this indicator is low, they note higher turnover, low productivity, and lower sales.

The fact that matters with emotional intelligence in the team are not working well is evidenced by frequent outbursts of employee anger, conflicts, a lack of understanding of the specifics of the work of neighboring departments and specific colleagues, as well as difficulties in interacting with customers and contractors. In american A 2005 study found that four out of five employees lost valuable working time worrying about an unpleasant incident, and more than half of those surveyed put off things, avoiding colleagues with whom they do not have an affair. Is the justification "no time for sharing" valid if, due to inattention to one's and others 'experiences, productivity drops so much?

In the book "Another mind. An expert in the study of emotional intelligence, Harvey Deutschendorf refers to data from a study at the Yale School of Management, according to which 24% of respondents report that they constantly feel annoyed at work. Deutschendorf notes that "employees can only give what they get themselves," and a healthy corporate culture is a direct path to satisfied customers.

It would seem that all these things, which sound like arguments "for everything good versus everything bad," are intuitively understood, which means that they do not require special skills and theoretical research. However, if everything was so simple, we would not fall into the same type of trap and would never lose our temper.

Consider several working situations in which the ability to understand genuine emotions and desires can do a good job.

The specialist takes too much

Problem. The employee or manager seeks to resolve all issues and delve into everything at once. Because of this, its performance drops, and at the time of the company's active growth, the problem is especially noticeable.

Decision. In such a situation, it is important for a specialist to acknowledge their experiences that impede the delegation of authority: for example, fear of losing control or an excessive desire for approval, which leads to unproductive perfectionism. The authors of the book "Inspirational Leader: Team. The meanings. Energy "Jan Mulfeit and Melina Kosti cite statistics according to which" 80% of managers were not aware of their own skills and talents. " According to the authors, a successful leader knows his gaps and surrounds himself with employees who complement him and each other. A high level of self-knowledge allows you to formulate your own strengths and weaknesses in order to do what works best and not waste resources in vain.

Meetings end in quarrels

Problem. Discussions within the team lead to disagreements and even scandals because different members of the team have different points of view.

Decision.An important question that lies in the field of emotions: why is there really a quarrel? Professionals are considered to be "adults," which means they should not be offended or come from a spirit of contradiction. But it was not there! We will unlock and rationalize to the last, asserting: "I'm not upset at all, just my strategy is better." However, often behind these words lies disappointment due to the fact that our ideas (and therefore ourselves) were not appreciated. As a result, a person does not notice how he begins to juggle the facts in order to be right. Therefore, it is important for each participant in the discussion:

1) to ask himself where what he is confident as professional ends in and what he upholds in order to win the dispute;

2) to understand where this boundary passes with the opponent.

Customer wants strange

Problem. Is it possible to fulfill the wishes of the client, and at the same time, create a quality product if the conditions seem strange and difficult to fulfill?

Decision. To successfully negotiate, you need to be a bit of a psychologist: we all often don't realize what we really want. Suppose a client comes with samples, showing them as an example of successful execution, but it's obvious to the developers that there are much more modern and interesting solutions. You can agree and make a product for which you will be ashamed, or enter into a dispute, starting from specific details, and possibly lose your client. However, the main thing is to understand what exactly the other side likes in the examples given and to help formulate the request correctly. It is very likely that the most valuable is not an outdated design or unsuccessful technical execution, but something completely different. Having found the main value, you can correctly set the task.

Thus, modern science does not push experience into the background, but carefully studies. At the same time, emotional intelligence is attributed to the mandatory qualities of professionals, and its development - to practices that are important for successful work.

Emotional Intelligence And Managerial Leadership Style

Emotions are an evolutionarily earlier mechanism for regulating behavior than the mind. Therefore, they choose simple ways to solve life situations. To those who follow their "advice", emotions add energy. Under the strong influence of emotions in the body, such a mobilization of forces takes place that the mind cannot cause either orders or requests.

Convinced that the struggle with emotions brings the winner more thorns than laurels, people tried to find ways to influence their emotional world that would allow them to penetrate into the deep mechanisms of experiences and use these mechanisms more intelligently than nature ordered them to.

Little joys of life are necessary to compensate for unpleasant experiences, but one should not expect deep satisfaction from their sum. It is known that children who are deficient in parental affection are drawn to sweets. One candy can relieve stress in a child for some time, but even a large number of them cannot make him happier.

Each of us is somewhat reminiscent of a child reaching for candy when he tries to influence his emotions right at the moment of their occurrence. The short-term effect obtained by situational control of emotions cannot lead to stable emotional balance. This is due to the stability of the overall emotionality of a person.

The problem of human emotional culture has remained relevant throughout the history of human society. Back in the Bible, in the Book of Proverbs, we find examples of the emotional wisdom of mankind: "A meek answer averts anger, and an insulting word excites" ; "Slow to anger is better than the mighty, and owns a better taketh a city" .

Ecclesiastes teaches: "lamentation is better than laughter; because with sorrow of the face the heart is made better" Following philosophers of antiquity, modern philosophers emphasize the urgency of the problem of developing emotional competence - a person's openness to his emotional experiences, linking its capabilities with the harmonious interaction of the heart and mind, affect and intelligence.

In a modern civilized society, the number of people suffering from neurosis is constantly growing. The solution to the problem of emotional disorders could be facilitated by focused work on the development of emotional wisdom, the ability that is called emotional intelligence in modern foreign and domestic studies.

Recently, the term "emotional intelligence" is becoming increasingly popular.

For the first time the designation EQ - coefficient of emotionality was introduced in 1985 by the clinical physiologist Ruven Bar-On. In 1990, John Mayer and Peter Salovey introduced the concept of "emotional intelligence." Together with Daniel Goleman, the most famous in our country, these scientists make up the "top three" in studies of emotional intelligence. There are many definitions of emotional intelligence.

Ruven Bar-On, author of the abbreviation EQ, for example, defines emotional intelligence as "a set of non-cognitive abilities, competencies and skills that affect a person's ability to cope with challenges and environmental pressures."

Russian researcher D.V. Lucin, starting from existing concepts, offers his own model. Emotional intelligence is understood by him as the ability to understand and control their own and others' emotions.

From a psychologist view, emotional intelligence is the ability to recognize one's emotions and the emotions of another, the ability to control one's emotions and the emotions of another and build our interaction on this basis.

High emotional intelligence in itself may not be a reliable predictor of success in work. However, it serves as the basis for the competencies that are necessary for success.

Emotional competenceassociated with and based on emotional intelligence. The level of emotional intelligence is necessary for training specific competencies related to emotions. For example, the ability to clearly recognize what another person feels makes it possible to develop competencies such as the ability to influence and inspire other people.

Similarly, it is easier for people who are better able to control their emotions to develop competencies such as initiative and the capacity to work in stressful situations.

It is the analysis of emotional competencies that is necessary to predict success in work. It was on the basis of mental and technical abilities that a person's prospects for success in life were evaluated. Our people before the Americans doubted the correctness of this theory, asking the question: "If you are so smart, then why so poor?"

In his book, Daniel Goleman presented research data, according to which IQ in different versions affects a person's success with a probability of 4 to 25%. Goleman explains this by the fact that in order to get into managers, it is necessary to have a certain level of IQ (intelligence coefficient). You need it in order to go to university, for example. Therefore, all managers have a certain level of IQ. And in order to climb the career ladder, you need already something else.

When in numerous studies they compared how successful managers differ from average managers, studies began to point to other kinds of abilities related to understanding and managing emotions.

The theory of emotional intelligence in the first months stunned businessmen, refuting one of the main ideas of success in the twentieth century: "Emotions have no place at work." In his book, Goleman convincingly proves that people who combine reason and feelings are most effective in their activities . It is people with high emotional intelligence who make better decisions, act more effectively in critical situations and better manage their subordinates, which, accordingly, contributes to their growth in the ranks.

Even 100 years before our era, the philosopher Pablius Sirus said: "Manage your feelings until your senses begin to control you."

Emotions carry a huge layer of information, using which we can act much more effectively. An important point in this approach is that emotional intelligence allows you to control your emotions. The attractiveness of the emotional intelligence approach is that managing emotions is a skill that can be developed and developed, which is currently confirmed by research data.

The words of the outstanding leader "Personnel decide everything" accurately describe the realities of the modern world. In the conditions of fierce competition, the most successful companies with competent employees. Since in managerial processes the main role is given to interaction between people, competence in the field of interpersonal relations comes to the fore.

What abilities should a person have in order to successfully build relationships with others, in order to achieve success not only in his personal life, but also in his professional activity?

A number of studies conducted by scientists around the world show that these abilities are related to understanding and controlling emotions.

In 1990, John Mayer and Peter Salovey introduced the concept of "emotional intelligence." What does this concept include?

Emotional intelligence serves as the basis for emotional competence, which includes four competencies. The high level of development of which ensures career advancement.

So let's call them:

- Awareness of your emotions.
- Manage your emotions.

- Awareness of other people's emotions.
- Controlling the emotions of other people.

Since the 20th century, the first studies of emotionality have been conducted. Since then, it is generally accepted that emotional people are distinguished by the fact that everyone takes to heart and reacts violently to trifles, while unemotional people have an enviable composure.

The famous Soviet psychophysiologist V.D. Nebylitsyn considered emotionality to be one of the main components of a person's temperament and singled out characteristics such as sensitivity , impulsivity (speed and thoughtlessness of emotional reactions), lability (dynamism of emotional states).

Depending on the temperament, a person with a greater or lesser intensity is emotionally involved in various situations. But if emotionality is directly related to temperament, which is based on the properties of the nervous system, then the ability to intelligently control emotionality without interfering with physiological processes is extremely doubtful.

Can a choleric reasonably regulate the intensity of his outbreaks, if impulsivity prevails in his temperament - a tendency to quick and thoughtless emotional reactions? He will have time to "break firewood" for nothing, before he realizes that the most reasonable principle of managing emotions is balance.

And an unflappable phlegmatic person who is not capable of vividly and directly demonstrating his feelings will always be perceived by others as a person who is deeply indifferent to what is happening. If emotionality is understood only as a combination of strength, speed of occurrence and mobility of emotional reactions, then one area of application remains for the mind: to accept that there are emotional and unemotional people, and to reckon with their natural features.

In itself, this mission of the mind is extremely important for human understanding. Features of temperament must be taken into account in various communication situations. For example, do not be offended by the violent reaction of the choleric, which more often testifies to his impulsiveness than to the conscious intention to offend the interlocutor.

He can be answered in the same way, without risking a long conflict, but even one harsh word can permanently unbalance a melancholic - a vulnerable and impressionable person with a heightened sense of dignity.

To learn how to reasonably relate to the peculiarities of the emotional state of other people, it is not enough to know these features, you also need to control yourself , to maintain balance regardless of how intense your own emotional reactions are. Such an opportunity arises in the event that from fruitless attempts to directly influence the intensity of emotions, a person switches to managing situations in which emotions arise and manifest.

The emotional resources of a person are not unlimited, and if in some situations they are spent too generously, in others their deficiency begins to be felt. Even hyperemotional people who seem to be inexhaustible to others in the manifestation of their feelings, while in a calm environment, are immersed in a inhibited state to a greater extent than those who are classified as unemotional.

Emotions, as a rule, do not arise spontaneously, they are attached to situations and turn into stable states if the situation persists for a long time. Such emotions are called passion. And the more important one life situation is for a person, the higher the probability that one passion will supplant all the others.

Only great passion, claimed the French writer Henri Petit, is able to tame our passions. And his compatriot, writer Victor Cherbullier drew attention to the possibility of the opposite effect, arguing that our passions devour each other, and often large devour small ones.

It is generally accepted that in youth a person is emotional, and with age, emotionality is largely lost. In fact, with the accumulation of life experience, a person expands the spheres of emotional involvement, more and more situations cause him emotional associations, and, therefore, each of them causes a less intense reaction.

The overall emotionality remains the same, although in each situation observed by others, a person behaves more restrained than in his youth. Of course, there are cases when even with age the ability to react vigorously and continuously to certain events is not lost. But this is typical for people of a fanatical warehouse who concentrate their emotions in one particular area and absolutely do not pay attention to what and how is happening in others.

At every moment of time, a person experiences some kind of emotion. Think about what emotion you are currently experiencing (your physical condition and internal dialogue serve as an indicator of emotions). What is its intensity? How often does your emotion change? What emotions prevail in you?

If the answers to these questions did not cause you any difficulties, then you are clearly guided in the world of your emotions. Awareness of the emotions of others involves the ability to understand the emotions that other people experience, according to their verbal and non-verbal behavior, and also the ability to differentiate the true and false manifestations of the feelings of other people, to determine the change in the intensity of emotions and transitions from one emotion to another.

Managing your emotions - the ability to determine the source and cause of the emotion, its purpose and possible consequences of development, the degree of its usefulness in a particular situation, we can regulate emotions by controlling breathing, the state of the body, using verbal and non-verbal methods, controlling internal dialogue. The ability to evoke the emotion necessary in a particular situation belongs to the same skill. This skill helps actors get used to the image.

Another example of how important it is to have this skill. What determines the result in sports? Of course from the skill of the athlete. Yes, but not only. How many times have we observed the failures of the strongest. "I could not cope with the excitement," say sports commentators in such cases. Indeed, the result depends on how well the athlete knows how to control his own emotions .

Will the shooter hit the target or the hand will tremble, can the skater perform the crucial jump cleanly, or, say, the weightlifter "take the weight" ?. In training, they did this thousands of times, everything was worked out in the smallest details and brought to automatism, and at the crucial moment they lose their nerves. It is not in vain that they say that sports competition is a competition of nerves.

Emotional competence includes the management of other people's emotions . And it involves the ability to determine the possible cause of the emotion of another person and to assume the consequences of its development, a change in the state of another person using verbal and non-verbal means; the ability to evoke the right emotion in people.

When you tell a joke, you want to arouse the positive emotion of your interlocutor (verbal remedy). In a situation where a person experiences fear, he may not say this, everyone will say for him his facial expressions, posture, intonation (this is a non-verbal manifestation). Many talented artists, poets, musicians control our emotions through their works.

Much has been said and written about staff motivation. But somehow it happened that in practice the motivation system is reduced sometimes only to a differentiated system of remuneration: you do more and better - you get more, you do less and worse - you get less. This works, at least in most cases.

But is this enough today? After all, the situation on the labor market has changed significantly in recent years.

If earlier employers chose employees from a large number of candidates, today, more and more often, employees themselves choose the most suitable working conditions for themselves, the most suitable companies. Especially if they are qualified specialists, the lack of which is already felt well in the market. And they are no longer just one high salary and a good social package. They choose companies where they can most fully satisfy their emotional needs: respect, recognition, status, comfort. It is noted that the higher the social status of a person, the more attention he pays to satisfy his emotional needs.

The similar can be said of those who already work in the company. I must admit that people decide whether to stay with them or not, guided solely by emotions.

Employees remain in the company if their manager manages to create a comfortable atmosphere. And the decision is extremely emotional.

There are many examples where employees left high-paying jobs just because they did not receive moral satisfaction. And vice versa, they remained at work at a low salary, if they were completely satisfied with everything else, that is, they were emotionally satisfied.

If a person feels emotional discomfort, then sooner or later he will leave the company. If he still remains, then his productivity will be very far from that which he is really capable of. After all, the energy of employees aimed at work depends not only on the size of wages, it's widely depends on how he feels.

It should be noted here that the difference in the productivity of employees sometimes has nothing to do with their knowledge and skills. Everything is based on their emotional state and work efficiency depends on how they feel when doing it.

It's simple: if a person wants to work well, he works. If he does not want to, he does not try to work and does not use his full potential. The motivation task is precisely that the person wants to work well. And material incentives alone are clearly not enough.

As practice shows, material incentives quite well motivate for some time. But sooner or later, the employee needs to be proud of his work, there is a need for recognition of his merits by management and colleagues. In other words, there will be a need for emotional factors of motivation. And if he does not get what he wants, then his productivity will inevitably decline.

Emotional discomfort inevitably leads to reduced productivity. The employee simply does not see the point of working in full force. In extreme cases, such discomfort can cause overt sabotage and the loss of a valuable employee for the company. In the zone of emotional comfort, people work easily, with pleasure and do their job well. It`s naturally. Each person subconsciously seeks positive emotions.

People learn and work best when they are in a good mood, when they are interested. In this case, they mobilize their full potential. And after that they most of all want the circumstances in which they enjoyed to be repeated.

Negative emotions, on the contrary, reduce working capacity, worsen mental activity, reduce the ability to concentrate, and, as a result, reduce productivity . No matter how efficient the employee is, when factors appear in his environment or in his mind that prevent him from feeling good and comfortable while working, his efficiency decreases several times, and the situation itself causes a rejection reaction.

Meanwhile, one of the main tasks of any manager is precisely to fully utilize the full potential of their employees in their work. That is what all work aimed at motivating staff is aimed at.

Increasing productivity and, as a result, profitability is the result of introducing a competent motivation system. And here it is not possible to do without managing the emotional sphere. A manager, if he wants to be truly effective, must be able to manage emotions, both his own and his employees.

A competent manager, before asking a question: "How to get more return from subordinates?", Should ask himself a question: "How to change their emotions in the direction necessary for the business?".

It would seem that everyone knows this. Indeed, there is nothing fundamentally new here. But in practice, few people do at least something in this area. The management style remains the same: instructions, directives, instructions. Emotional competence is perceived by the leader as something insignificant, and sometimes completely unnecessary. Well, and those managers who are aware of the need for change, unfortunately, do not always know what needs to be done.

Indeed, what can be done to make the work more interesting, exciting, stimulating activity for employees? How to create an atmosphere of trust and support? The question is not simple.

First of all, you should stop treating employees as a work tool. A worker is not a soulless mechanism, it is a living person. And this means that he has emotions whether we want it or not. And on what emotions he experiences at work, his dedication and his productivity largely depend.

Leaders of all ranks should understand that the ability to positively affect the emotions of an employee increases the efficiency of his work, improves his relations with colleagues, interaction with clients. Recognizing the effect of emotions on labor productivity is the first step, followed by others.

Personnel management must necessarily affect emotional factors. Times are changing, and the directive management style is gradually becoming a thing of the past. There are a lot of options for influencing the emotional sphere of employees; you just need to want to start changes in this area.

The business world is changing rapidly. The labor market is also changing. The ability to develop any company lies in the ability to find and retain qualified specialists, talented employees.

Material incentives certainly play a big role. But emotional factors are beginning to play an increasing role. And the further, the more their role will increase. Only a comprehensive motivation system with the obligatory consideration of the emotional component will allow employees to achieve full dedication at work, maximum efficiency and productivity.

Managing a team of employees is one of the most important tasks of any organization. To ensure the highest efficiency of his activities, along with formal managerial functions, the leader should play the role of a motivator and moral leader, increasing the interest and efficiency of his subordinates, as well as maintaining an optimal atmosphere in the team.

Interest in the social and emotional aspects of work arose in science back in the 20s of the last century. It was noted that the more interest and participation in the problems of his subordinates the head shows, the higher the satisfaction of employees with their work.

Most of the competencies necessary for the success of a leader have a social and emotional nature. In a modern organization, the leader, undoubtedly, is faced with the task of creating a favorable atmosphere in the team, directing collective emotions in the right direction, since the productivity of the group's work largely depends on the success of this function.

An effective leader not only varies the styles of his leadership depending on the situation, but is also able to apply a variety of skills related to emotional intelligence.

Numerous studies of modern psychologists are devoted to finding the optimal leadership model, and most of them focus on external and group criteria for leadership effectiveness. In other words, the ultimate result of the work of the entire team, which includes the contributions of all employees, acts as a criterion for the effectiveness of the leader's activities.

Sources for the selection of performance criteria can serve as indicators of labor productivity, estimated data and information about the staff. However, such indicators can be associated with many other factors related not only to the activities of a particular leader, but also to the characteristics of the organization as a whole. In addition, an indicator of the effectiveness of the leader is the attitude of his subordinates to each other and to himself - in particular.

Successful performance by a manager of his functions helps to increase psychological comfort, which includes satisfaction with the activity and its results, satisfaction with the psychological climate in the team, and the adequacy of professional identification and self-esteem.

At the same time, the working conditions of the leader and the tasks facing him pose the greatest threat to maintaining psychological comfort. So, the leader is faced with a constant assumption of responsibility, the need to continuously maintain his authority in the eyes of colleagues and subordinates, to maintain emotional contact with them.

The consequence of such working conditions may be the so-called phenomenon of emotional burnout, expressed in the "damping" of emotions, the disappearance of the severity of feelings and feelings, an increase in the number of conflicts with communication partners, indifference and fencing off from the experiences of others, loss of a sense of the value of life, loss of faith in one's own strength .

The opposite of emotional burnout is considered a state of enthusiasm for work. This condition is characterized by cheerfulness, energy, enthusiasm, preoccupation with activity and a sense of effective inclusion in the life of the organization. It is enthusiasm for work that contributes to the successful performance of employee functions.

The term "burnout" was introduced in 1974 by the American psychiatrist H. Freidenberger. Initially, this concept was defined as a state of exhaustion, mental fatigue, exhaustion with a sense of personal futility, apathy, unwillingness to continue to work, which, undoubtedly, reduces the effectiveness of the activity.

The employees of medical institutions and various charitable organizations were recognized as susceptible to "emotional burnout". In a broad sense, burnout is an affective reaction to chronic stress that occurs during the work of professionals who are constantly faced with people who are in trouble, need help and support.

In the 80s, the risk category was expanded. Now it includes teachers, psychologists, lawyers, politicians, sellers, leaders of all levels, that is, representatives of professions such as "person-person". The content of the activities of these professionals varies greatly, but all of them are united by the subject of their work, the need for close contact with people, which from an emotional point of view is often difficult to maintain for a long time.

Recently, emotional intelligence is increasingly seen as one of the factors for effective team leadership.

Today, most executives recognize that emotion is certainly important in building relationships with colleagues, subordinates, partners, and customers. But not everyone thinks about the influence of their emotions on daily decisions.

In order to successfully manage their subordinates, each leader must first of all understand that the subordinate is "the other". In an organization, everything cannot be the same; the "other" is a managerial necessity.

If all employees are creative people, then who will do the routine? Who will create team relationships? If all employees are the same, then there is no resource for development.

In order for the team to be successful, it is necessary to select its employees not for themselves, but in accordance with the task.

It is always dangerous to ignore the feelings of people in organizations, as well as to neglect any real facts. Therefore, for any manager, both their own emotions and the feelings of subordinates should be the object of attention.

Depending on the chosen management strategy, the manager will treat his employees differently: in one case, attention to the feelings of subordinates is necessary, since this gives you a very effective tool for manipulation, in the other, feelings become one of the forms of feedback, an indicator of the organization's state.

The possibility of a regular open exchange of feelings in the organization is necessary for the leader to timely adjust his actions.

Organization is an association of people having common goals, which cannot be achieved by any of them without the help of others.

At the same time, any person achieves his personal goals: to provide himself with the necessary income, career growth, to participate in solving problems that fully reveal his own potential. The property of the human community is that all people are unique, they have different motives and goals, which means that with any form of association, personal interests will be objective facts in any organization. But the unconsciousness of these interests and the inability to formulate them leads to instability in behavior, problems in business interaction.

To determine by what principle it is necessary to build relationships with his subordinates, the manager must first recognize his personal goals and interests, answer the question: "Why do I need this organization, what do I want from it," and then help my employees realize the goals and choose a way to manage them in order to more effectively implement their goals, and their goals, and the organization as a whole.

The more styles in the manager's arsenal, the better. The best climate and the highest performance indicators are observed in those companies whose leaders manage with the help of several styles, but with a predominance, nevertheless, of a democratic leadership style.

The most successful leaders are able to almost imperceptibly move from one style to another depending on the situation. The more interest and participation in the problems of his subordinates the head shows, the higher the satisfaction of employees with their work.

Conclusion

Criticism focuses primarily on the term "emotional intelligence" and on the question of how it fits in with the traditional constructs of intelligence and complements them meaningfully. In terms of content, the concept describes highly relevant human abilities. These are discussed in Science under the headings "Emotion Regulation" or "self-regulation." Whether the term "emotional intelligence" will prevail in science should primarily depend on how far it is possible to validate this concept by appropriate tests and to distinguish it theoretically from other psychological constructs.

Heiner Rindermann made an attempt in this direction in the German-speaking area with the questionnaire for measuring emotional competence. This test for the operationalization and empirical verification of this concept is based on a norm sample of more than 600 persons and achieves - according to the author - satisfactory values in terms of validity and reliability. He further suggests that the term intelligence should be reserved for cognitive abilities and should not be overstretched, especially as the correlation between emotional competences and (cognitive) intelligence is not high. The test collects four dimensions of emotional competencies, namely the ability to

(1) Recognize one's feelings,

(2) To recognize the feelings of others,

(3) To regulate one's feelings, and

(4) To express emotions as emotional expressivity.

In terms of the relevance and importance of the topic (whether emotional intelligence or emotional competence), empirical studies show that people who have the ability to control their own and others' emotions are more successful in their professional and private lives; they are less prone to mental disorders, have better personal relationships, are happier and less susceptible to unfavorable habits such as smoking, unhealthy eating, etc. For example, a 2011 meta-analysis found that emotional intelligence is more related to career success as cognitive intelligence and the five personality dimensions. Further research results on the topics that supplement or continue the concept of emotional intelligence can be found in the articles Emotions regulation and Volition.

In the nineteenth century, what today is called " Emotional Intelligence " (in the opinion of Ute Frevert) is not in the context of psychological science, but in the context of a theological-moral discourse, in educational theory, or in literature been treated. In this context, heart formation actually appears as a counterpart to intelligence, as expressed for example in the usual phrase "intellect and heart"

Remember, what will help to form emotional intelligence:

1. Self-knowledge

Psychologists argue that current experiences are a reflection of an earlier emotional experience. This means that your ability to perceive anger, sadness, fear and joy most likely depends on the quality and intensity of emotions in the early stages of life.

If in the past you appreciated and understood your emotions, they will become valuable assets in the future. If the experiences were painful and confusing, you will probably do your best to distance yourself from them. However, one should not even step aside from negative feelings, because the acceptance and awareness of one's emotional state is the key to understanding how experiences affect your thoughts and actions.

Here are the surest ways to improve self-knowledge:

Train your mindfulness. That is, the intentional focus on the present. Awareness is often associated with meditation in Buddhism, but most religions in the world practice something similar in the form of prayer. She removes anxiety, calms and tunes, educates character.

Keep a diary. At the close of each day, pen down what happened to you, how you felt and coped with difficulties. Periodically look back and analyze typical situations, note where you did not finish the press or overdo it.

Ask loved ones how they see you. Reviews from a few people will reveal your strengths and weaknesses. Do not forget to fix everything and find patterns. The main thing is not to argue or object. It is important for you to look at yourself through the eyes of others.

2. Self-control

Awareness of feelings is the first step towards emotional management. You must use emotions to make constructive decisions and build a line of behavior. When you become overly tense, you can lose control of yourself and lose thoughtfulness.

Remember, it is easy to think rationally in a state of overvoltage. Probably not. This is because the brain is detached from thought processes and switches to an overabundance of feelings.

3. Empathy

We constantly focus on what is most important for us. However, our emotions are only half the relationship. All other people also have their own feelings, desires, triggers and fears. Therefore, empathy is an extremely important life skill.

Try some practical tips to help you become empathic:

Speak less, listen more. This is the golden rule of any truly empathic person. Of course, you cannot let the whole gamut of the feelings of another person through you, but you can try to hear it. Just let the person speak out without interrupting them with their thoughts. This is difficult, especially if there are strong negative emotions. However, almost any connection will become stronger only because you will wait an extra few seconds before entering into a conversation.

Accept the opposite opinion contrary to your own position. To understand what drives a person, you need to be in his place. If you think your boss is reckless, try to justify him in your head. Perhaps you would have done the same if you found yourself in his shoes.

Understand the difference between the words "I know" and "I understand you." The first indicates that you supposedly had a similar life experience. The second one says that you thought about the situation and lost it on your behalf. Of course, understanding other people's problems is a more trusting and truthful level of relationship.

Empathy implies your reaction, but it must arrive on time. If someone is ready to burst into tears or burst with deep pain, do not try to muffle feelings. A person must throw out emotions, and he will need your help.

4. Motivation

When we talk about motivation as a component of emotional intelligence, we mean an inner core, not psychological forces, to lift our body out of bed.

The goal can be a career, family, a work of art, and anything else, if only it has significant significance in your life. When motivation is set to work, it combines with reality, and we commit real actions. To start a family, motivated people start dating. To advance in service, motivated people undertake self-education.

How to find your rod?

First, you need to find out your own values. Many of us are so busy that we do not have time to delve into ourselves and determine priorities. Even worse, if a person does work that directly contradicts his worldview and principles.

Secondly, it is worth transferring your goal to paper and paint it in detail. It is necessary to understand that great success is greatly extended over time. It consists of small victories and bitterness of defeat.

5. Social skills

Social skills are the ability to understand the non-verbal signals that people around you constantly address to you. These signals give a clear idea of what a person is experiencing and what is really important for him. In order to receive non-verbal signals, it is necessary to suspend your thoughts, not think about the goals and objectives that you pursue, being next to a person.

Emotional intelligence is the key to successful interaction with other people. Invest in emotional intelligence!